All Those *Pieces*

Into the Hearts and Minds of the
Psychologically Stranded

A Memoir

JESSICA WISLEY

Copyright © 2020 Jessica Wisley
All rights reserved
First Edition

PAGE PUBLISHING, INC.
Conneaut Lake, PA

First originally published by Page Publishing 2020

This is a work of creative non-fiction. The author has recreated events and conversations from memory. In order to maintain anonymity, names of characters, locations, and identifying characteristics have been changed.

ISBN 978-1-6624-0132-9 (pbk)
ISBN 978-1-6624-0133-6 (digital)

Printed in the United States of America

To all the developmentally disabled and to all who have served them.

Contents

Definitions 7
Prologue 9
Introduction 11

Part One: Into the Fire 23
Chapter 1:   Alter Ego 25
Chapter 2:   See Jane Run 36
Chapter 3:   It's Only a Delusion 45
Chapter 4:   I've Got Your Number 52
Chapter 5:   On the Warpath 58
Chapter 6:   Hear No Evil, Speak No Evil 64
Chapter 7:   The Gang's All Here 71
Chapter 8:   A Different Plane 84
Chapter 9:   The Show Must Go On 91

Part Two: Out to the Frying Pan 101
Chapter 10: On the Tip of My Tongue 103
Chapter 11: Matter Over Mind 111
Chapter 12: Tickle Me Pink 122
Chapter 13: No Ray of Hope 136
Chapter 14: Let's Play Charades 141
Chapter 15: That's Hard to Swallow 146
Chapter 16: It's Just a Game 153
Chapter 17: All in Good Faith 161

Epilogue	169
Afterword	175
Acknowledgements	179
Appendices	181
Glossary	185
Sources	203

/ saɪkəˈlɑdʒɪkli /

Psychologically

Pertaining to the mind or to mental phenomena; cognitive, conceptual, abstract

> /ˈstrændɪd /
>
> Stranded
>
> Lacking what is necessary to leave a place or to get out of a situation; helpless, homeless, isolated, passed up
>
> Composed of a specified number of strands; threaded, pieced, strung

Prologue

Strolling into the large classroom to retrieve one of my students, I glimpsed her out of the corner of my eye. I immediately knew something bad was on the way. She was still seated but bore a look of sheer animal rage. As she jumped up and leapt toward me, I had just enough time to lift my right arm to shield my face (as I had been taught to do). She clamped down so fiercely on my forearm that she and I essentially became one. Her teeth cut into me as she threw me up against a desk. Time seems to freeze in such moments. I remember falling back on the desk, completely unable to move. The next thing I remember is feeling a release as a large woman pulled her off of me. I was left half dazed. Her teeth had left their imprint on my arm, and I was bleeding…

Introduction

I went back for my final college degree later in life, well after venturing into other various careers. In my twenties, I was active duty in the U.S. Air Force, which included a two-year station in Great Britain. Previously, I had gone to school for a biology degree. After my military discharge, I spent a few years working in a number of different labs. More specifically, I had run drug analyses on postmortem blood samples in the medical examiner's lab. I had also tested water as an environmental technician, and later I worked as a chemist for a company that formulated liquid cleansing products.

By my early thirties, I had become dissatisfied. It was not that I didn't like or appreciate my different jobs. Rather, it was that I began to feel the loss of not making a real *impact* in anybody's life. This feeling continued to gnaw at me, to the point where I realized a dramatic change was in order.

At thirty-three, I essentially started all over again. I went back to school for a master's degree to become a speech-language pathologist (SLP). It was another grueling three-and-a-half full-time years of college, but I wouldn't have done it any differently if even given the chance. It was so worth it—all the effort, the finances, and the complete upheaval of my life. My only employment during those years was within the Air National Guard (which I had joined two years after my active duty discharge).

After graduation, I spent another three years working with children in a school (most ages five to ten), and I loved it. (In fact, I had told a friend later that the experience had been "my finest hour.") I was merely a long-term substitute, however, and when the permanent SLP returned, I was out of a job. Unemployed within my career field, I found available school speech therapist jobs in short supply where I lived.

I contemplated even relocating to Alaska, where I was sure I could work in my desired field. To try it out, I took a month's speech therapist assignment servicing children in remote Alaskan schools. I spent two weeks in the Northwest Arctic and two weeks in the Aleutian Islands. It was the experience of a lifetime. I decided in the end, however, that I didn't *really* desire to dwell amidst grizzly bears, nor did I *really* want to endure winters that were eight months long.

While I was still in Alaska, I received a voicemail at home that would forever change my course. I was offered an SLP position at an agency that serviced developmentally-disabled adults. Though I was in no hurry to commit anywhere, the rest is history, because I really needed the job.

*****

Developmental disabilities (DDs) are chronic conditions due to mental and/or physical impairments that arise before the age of eighteen. DDs usually cause difficulties in areas of life such as independent living, language, learning, mobility, and the helping of oneself. Some of the more common DDs are Down syndrome, fetal alcohol spectrum disorders, autism spectrum disorders (ASDs), intellectual disability (ID), and cerebral palsy.

ASDs are a group of DDs that lead to significant social, communicative, and behavioral challenges, and include both Heller's and Asperger's syndromes. IDs are characterized by significant limitations in both intellectual functioning (general mental capacity, such as reasoning, problem-solving, and learning) and adaptive behavior (which covers many everyday social and practical skills).

A higher-functioning DD person is usually one who operates on a more advanced level than a lower-functioning individual does. Often, such a person masks the symptoms of the DD, thereby passing as the "norm."

Most of the individuals placed in our agency carry more than one diagnosis; this includes mental illness diagnoses as well. For example, an individual might be secondarily diagnosed with schizoaffective disorder, intermittent explosive disorder, or post-traumatic stress disorder (PTSD). Additionally, there was an entire sex-offender unit for those who had entered our agency by order of the regional courts.

How did I feel about taking this new position? My neighbor told me that a friend had told him the agency would be "a very hard place to work." I took that as neither here nor there. I will admit I was somewhat nervous about the entire sex-offender thing. At the time I began my job, I pictured all such individuals as rapists one might encounter in a back-alley's darkest end. I found later my assumption had been wrong.

I had experienced only one college externship servicing DD adults. I had done very well in that setting, despite the initial shock. (I had been taken aback by proximity to such people unable to control their very drives.) So then, apart from the sex-offender issue, I was generally open-minded about giving it a go. I knew little of what to expect.

The beginning of my career required working on a campus, also known as the "grounds." It housed about two hundred people in all. The residents on the campus lived in small "cottages" with maybe twenty-five or so on each lot. The grounds also contained a schoolhouse, which in turn contained a bowling alley, a chapel, a gymnasium, an auditorium, and a pool. Each workday, the residents reported to either the schoolhouse, where they attended daily programs within classrooms, or to one of a few prevocational workshops on the site.

ALL THOSE PIECES

Every individual cottage was divided into three units. Each unit contained several bedrooms, two or three bathrooms, a common living area, a dining room, and a kitchen. Nearly every person on the campus had his or her own bedroom. Floors were vinyl, but other effects served to aid in a "homey" feel. The rooms contained nice furniture, pretty bedding, and personal mementos (posters, pictures, trophies, etc.) on the dressers and on the walls. Most of the residents had televisions in their rooms. There were occasions in which TVs had to be covered with Plexiglas and bedroom walls and floors required pads. This was due to the risk of property destruction and/or self-injurious behavior (also known as SIB).

Each particular unit varied in level of security. Some were complete "lockdown" units because their residents were high-risk for leave without consent. Others did not have to be locked, because there was no real need for them to be so. Depending upon its residents, and the varying risks of physical assault and/or aggression, some kitchens had to lock up "sharps." This included not only steak knives and scissors, but butter knives and table forks as well. As such prohibitions are considered rights restrictions, a special committee had to be summoned before they took effect. The committee made rulings as to the adherence to constraints of certain rights.

Within the living units, birthdays were celebrated yearly, and at Christmas there were always gifts. Meals were usually of high quality, and it was not uncommon to have opportunities to attend ballgames, concerts, and dances. Other outings included eating at restaurants, attending the movies, going shopping, and volunteering at the SPCA. Many of the individuals participated in organized seasonal sporting activities, for instance, softball, basketball, and bowling. Home visits occurred for those who were lucky enough to have functional families who were also involved. Church services (on Saturday evenings) were offered, presided over by "Father Dan." Medical care was consistent and thorough, and I was truly impressed with this all.

As far as relationships between the residents, there appeared to be very little to none. To start with, there were gross differences in levels of functioning and intellectual quotient (IQ). Secondly, even if two people were at similar operating levels, their diagnoses were rarely conducive to making friends. On the other hand, most reached out or up to staff for bonding and affirmation, as well as for having their basic needs met.

Days in the campus classrooms were short and ran mid-morning to mid-afternoon. Each room was run by a specific staff member or teacher, who was assisted by a number of aides. A variety of activities occurred in the rooms, such as those involving art and music (special teachers for each were frequently brought in). Seasonal activities were common, such as decorating for and celebrating special days of the year. Often, school outings and field trips were offered too. Some of the class members participated in very simple academics, such as spelling, reading, and math. Box games and puzzles were frequent activities as well.

Data on specific objectives for each person were targeted on a daily basis. For example, target goals might include the independent washing of one's hands, closing the bathroom door while toileting, or exchanging a few conversational volleys with a peer.

There were many different jobs within the workshops. These included piecework, loading vending machines, applying shrink wrap, and sorting mail. Shredding, laminating, stuffing envelopes, and cleaning were also among the tasks. Some of our cleaning crews washed cars on the grounds, as well as scrubbed floors in churches, the local VFW, and hotels. A large group of our individuals spent their days copying medical records and charts onto flat sheets of microfilm. Hours and pay varied considerably from person to person, depending on each individual's specific case.

Before I go on, I would like to take a moment to recognize all direct care staff, job coaches, classroom teachers and aides. Not only in my agency, but in *all* agencies that service the DD, such staff carry monumental amounts of responsibility within their respective roles. Quite honestly, I believe they have some of the most taxing jobs that exist, mentally, physically, and otherwise. I salute and applaud them all.

My primary responsibility was (and still is) to administer communications (speech and language) services, most frequently in individual pull-out sessions. (I retrieve a student from either a classroom or a workshop and bring that person to my therapy room.) Some of the many target objectives in the field have involved pragmatic (practical) language, such as maintaining eye contact, using greetings and social exchanges, and developing conversational skills. I also focus on articulation (the actual speech sounds), reading, and spelling. Additionally, I have taught the communications portion of our new employee training. All new employees have learned (I hope) about the ins and outs of language and communications as a whole.

Any sign language I now know has been the result of teaching myself. As hard as it is to believe, sign language was not offered, much less obligatory, while obtaining my degree as an SLP. I've since addressed sign language skills with many of the individuals I've served, plus I've held countless beginning sign language classes for staff.

My other primary responsibility as an SLP involves addressing those who have impairments to eating and swallowing food. I am a part of a team making recommendations for those with such swallowing difficulties, and for those who have experienced choking and/or aspiration (entry of food or drink into the lungs). Very frequently we must modify diets, be it cutting food into smaller pieces or making liquids thick. I have also provided swallowing therapy at times.

The team is called the interdisciplinary feeding, eating, and swallowing team (IFEAST), which consists of an SLP, an occupational therapist (OT), and a registered dietitian (RD). Unquestionably, these duties have been the least favorite part of my job, and have been largely the ones that have challenged me the most. Downgrading diets is never fun, and especially not so when restrictions prevent people from consuming their favorite foods.

The vision of the overall agency is to "make every day a quality day." Specifically, objectives for individuals include personal growth through community inclusion, empowerment, learning, and choice. The tension caused by living in a structured, regulated environment can be very real, so the agency seeks to help diminish that stress.

Each person is assigned a treatment team, which includes: a treatment team leader a psychiatrist, a psychologist, an SLP, an OT, a physical therapist (PT), a registered nurse (RN), a licensed practical nurse (LPN), an RD, a social worker, an active treatment manager, and either a classroom teacher or a worksite coach.

A person-centered planning (PCP) method is idealized agency-wide. I say *idealized*, and not *utilized* because

I find *utilized* is not always the case. PCP, in theory, aims to make forefront each person's interests and goals. Whereas traditional planning emphasizes what the person *cannot* do, PCP focuses on each person's talents and gifts. Services are developed *around* the individual through PCP, as opposed to the matching of a person to an existing "clone." PCP calls for the individual, along with his or her support group, to formulate the most convincing action plan. The support group may consist of any involved family members, along with each member of the aforementioned treatment team. Again, PCP is an ideal and is not always put into play.

*****

As I now prepare to retire, I want to share the stories about the people within my agency, most of whom I serviced as an SLP, but sometimes knew in other ways. I have twenty years of experience as an SLP, and fifteen years working with the developmentally delayed. I believe I am a person not only to relay these stories of others, but to tell the stories well. This memoir is based on my firsthand accounts, observations, and interactions. To protect identities, names and physical descriptions have been changed, and I will not reveal the name of the actual place where I worked.

The first half of this book addresses time periods in the early years, when I serviced individuals living on the grounds in a more institutional-like fashion. The second half addresses times after we "de-institutionalized," and after the individuals moved out into community group homes. As nothing is exact, some of the settings in the stories overlap.

I promise, there will be catharses; these stories will make you laugh, and they will also make you cry. Perhaps you already know (as I have come to know) that fiction is far less captivating than fact. These are stories, both funny and sad, that deserve to be shared by all. I believe you will not only find these stories compelling, but that you will gain new insight into the many issues that the developmentally disabled face. Light will also be shed on the specific trials of working with people so very unique. I hope, however, that you will arrive at the same conclusions that I have: the developmentally disabled are ultimately of the same value, virtue, and importance as are we all. I believe that we as a people should remain compassionate and hopeful for *each and every one*. Here are my most salient memories—some somber, some amusing, and some an uncanny blend of both. May you experience a walk through their world and mine.

Part One

Into the Fire

Chapter 1

Alter Ego

One of my earliest and most memorable students was Charles. I say *student* because it was more fitting than *consumer* or *client* or whatever the latest term for our people was at that time. (Today we unofficially say, *our individuals*.) Charles was in his late twenties and was the first sex offender that I serviced, or to my knowledge, had ever known.

To this day, I'm not certain as to whether or not he had been abused himself while growing up. I did know, however, that he had come from a socioeconomically disadvantaged home. His father had lost his job at a local grocery store, and his mother, who was excessively overweight, was unemployed.

Charles was diagnosed with intermittent explosive disorder, impulse control disorder, personality disorder, oppositional defiant disorder, pedophilia, paraphilia, and moderate ID. He also had a bilateral hearing loss and a Harrington rod to treat his scoliosis, placed along his spine. If all these issues were not enough, he exhibited gynecomastia (enlarged male breasts). That no doubt did not help any self-consciousness issues he probably already had.

Charles's targets were usually young boys or adolescents, and he referred to them as "my victims." His behavior plan directed that he was to have no contact with minors. He was also not to look at any pictures, TV shows, or movies that portrayed kids. In the community, his behavior plan specified that he look away when he saw children or teens. From when I first met him, he seemed to be obsessed with the desire to move to a group home. It's as if he believed that if that were to happen, all of his troubles would magically disappear. I guess I can't blame him for hoping, as without hope there is no life.

Charles was ambulatory and verbal, but the ID was marked. He could write (at the very best) at the level of a five-year-old. He had to count on his fingers to complete the simplest of math. His speech was rapid and poor. He had all those things that one tends to make stereotypical assumptions about: thick glasses, left-handed, red hair, and so forth.

The first time I met Charles, he told me he had "raped a kid in the bathroom." His speech was so poor at that time that I wasn't even sure that's what he said. Trust me, however, it was true. This had happened at a facility for the "mentally retarded" (that's what they called ID at the time, though *mentally retarded* is now largely considered an offensive term). Charles said that the kid was deaf and couldn't talk. I was taken aback.

Can you imagine being that kid's parents, or even worse, that kid?

Charles was assigned to one of the workshops. He had initiated the idea of me helping him with his speech (he had asked staff to introduce us when I first began my job on the site). I would go get him routinely from the workshop to come to my room for class. We first began working on articulation, reading, and writing. Charles realized that if he slowed down his speech, he could be more easily understood. Generally, though, he continued to speak at a rapid pace.

I also wanted to give my students as real an academic experience as possible (Charles could not even tell me the planet on which we lived). We worked on geography, astronomy, math, and religion, as well as language and speech. I taped two huge maps on the wall: the United States map as well as the map of the entire world. Charles had some dyslexia, and wrote some of his letters backward. He liked to write personal letters, especially to his parents. When he would get close to the right margin on a page, I would say, "Move down to the next line." He would invariably continue on the original line, smooshing all the letters together, causing me to grit my teeth.

Charles's letters were corny, but I helped him with what he wanted to say, and I truly believed he wanted that bond with his folks. He told me his parents tore the letters up without reading them, but I'm not sure if that was even true. Our individuals lied a lot. Lied and coveted. As for reading, he could read a simple consonant-vowel-consonant (CVC) word such as *cat* or *dog*, but not for the life of him could he read a CCVC word, such as *grip* or *crib* or *sled*. Also, when he would finally be able to read a simple word, two seconds later he could not read it again. (I found this over and over with the ID students—that was the nature of the beast. Sometimes I wanted to beat my head against the wall.)

Charles also had difficulty hearing the differences between individual sounds. (The ability to hear such differences is a part of overall phonological awareness.) For example, he was confused between the sounds /r/, /w/, and /l/. His hearing loss contributed to that problem; unfortunately, the loss was not considered severe enough for him to qualify for a state-funded hearing aid.

Overall, Charles remained enthusiastic about speech therapy for a very long time. His independent reading and spelling skills *did* show some improvement over time. I helped him journal his feelings so that he could better understand his own thoughts, while learning to take more positive actions in his life. We worked on recognizing various food words so that he could more proficiently order from a menu. I brought the issue of his handwriting to Rachael, our OT. She picked him up on her own caseload, and his printing of capital letters dramatically improved. During the latter part of our time together, I prepared Charles with index cards which contained questions for him to pose when he was interviewing for various group homes.

One day, out of the blue, Charles started to tell me about his grandfather who had taken him fishing when he was a kid. (The grandfather had committed suicide a year or two before.) The way Charles summed it up was with, "My grandpa shot himself in the head, then I did what I did (raped the kid), and then I ended up here." I thought it profound that he was able to make and express that link. I felt for him when one day (and could think of no appropriate response) when in utter frustration he made the comment, "No one will ever understand the problems that I have." He knew where he stood.

Charles had a spiritual dimension as well. He had been raised a Mormon, and he told me once that his family had gone to Salt Lake City when he was young. I found out later this was a lie ("I joked you," he had told me), and I realized this was not the first time he had lied to me (again, lying was the operative trait). Charles attended our small campus Bible study, which I will describe in more detail as we progress. He asked me for an extra-large-print Bible (despite wearing eyeglasses, he still experienced visual impairment), and I obtained it for him to read in our class. He truly embraced the lessons about the Bible characters, and especially about Christ. In fact, on more than one occasion, we attended the campus Ash Wednesday service together like friends. As vile and repulsive as he was to the world, he grew on my heart over time. I actually liked him, and I thought we had developed a special bond.

Charles, however, was not possible to predict. His angry outbursts were frequent, and he got violent, attacked staff, and destroyed others' property as well as his own. He made statements to me like "I wanna go back to jail" (as so many of our individuals did at some point in time). He also told me he clearly wanted "out of this hellhole" for good.

I met Charles's parents at a case review once (they had traveled two hours to get to our site). They seemed like nice, normal people and were truly concerned about their son. Charles always impressed me at his case reviews. Despite his deficits, he always made himself articulate, not only with intelligibility but with what he actually had to say. He usually talked "with his hands." He longed for a normal life, a life where he could live on his own, drive a car, work a real job, and so forth. Sadly, that could never be. Because of his perpetual deviant nature, his parents remained his legal guardians, but ended up severing all personal ties.

I came up with what I thought was a brilliant idea to give Charles his own personal calendar, to help him keep track of his appointments and meetings. At first this was a success, and he was proud to carry his calendar in a briefcase of his own. Eventually though, he began to obsess over it, demanding hundreds or even thousands of calendar pages at a time. He kept a shopping list and a Christmas wish list too and began to obsess over all his potential gifts as well. Though at times hidden, the coveting always returned.

In our final days together, Charles became more and more demanding, aggressive, and even belligerent. He was constantly expecting "prizes" from me, and I was starting to be wary of us being alone in a room. Charles was very tall and very strong. I think we both realized our time had come to an end. I had been seeing him three times a week for about five years. Charles ultimately ended up quitting speech therapy for good. Life went on.

I hear that today Charles is involved with many different activities, including self-advocacy and arts and crafts. He is also an active participant in a new pre-vocational workshop. He remains at risk though, for inappropriate sexual behavior, and taking advantage of friendships in order to do so. Charles is still egocentric and manipulative, and in constant need of attention and praise.

Charles was certainly not what I had anticipated the day I signed up for the SLP courses in school. In fact, he was anything *but* what I had planned. I don't know what my reaction would have been if someone had told me years ago what I would really be doing, and with whom. Somehow, I doubt it would have been a positive response. From the world's view, he was truly the lowest of lowlifes. And yes, it sickened me that he harbored sexual desires toward kids. Nonetheless, I'd developed patience that I'd never dreamed was possible. Again, I really *liked* Charles, but ultimately, what had I been trying to do? He would never read or do math or identify our state on the map. Was I merely filling the role of the friend he'd never had? What did our five years together actually mean?

*****

I met Jerry also early in my tenure. Jerry was in his late teens and in the IEP (individual education program) class—better known as special education. He was good-looking with dark hair, tan skin, and a portly build. He also came from a very low socioeconomic level home, had been sexually abused by both parents, and abused likewise by friends of his mom and dad. Jerry had PTSD from what he had suffered, was visibly disturbed, and was as fragile as an eggshell. He was also diagnosed with moderate ID, and he had a tendency toward SIB. For example, he had attempted to insert a lightbulb into his rectum in an assorted number of ways.

Jerry had frequent stays in psychiatric hospitals, and his hands would often shake in therapy. His speech was very immature, and he was either unable or unwilling to use pronouns as he should. He resented the idea of having to come to speech class and would wail, "Me not a baby, me know how to talk!" He constantly said, "Her is," "Him is," etc. I worked on this with him until I was blue in the face, all to no avail. It grated on my nerves when he misused the pronouns, and he really *did* sound like a baby. Jerry could not read but was also very smart. He loved art, and like so many of our individuals, he was *very good* at art. He loved to color and draw. I liked Jerry, frailties and all.

I remember at one point wanting to put Charles and Jerry within a therapy group. When I first proposed the idea to Charles, he became instantly alarmed. He was startled and queried, "How old is Jerry?" He was really taking the steps to keep from putting himself into a bad place. That impressed me again with Charles. (I did not move forward with the creation of that particular group.)

All I knew about Jerry's perspective was that he felt love and responsibility for his mother but that he also hated his dad. Once, when it appeared as if his mother was not coming to his case review, Jerry had to be led out of the room in tears. Fortunately, it turned out that his mother *did* make it to that meeting. (The only other thing I remember from that meeting was his mother screaming, "I don't want my son on no stinkin' medication!")

Jerry's behavior varied. Once when he became aggressive in the classroom, he had to be restrained. Staff needed extra help to do this, and they called for such over the intercom. I ran into his room, which was right next to mine, and served as the fourth person in the "takedown," with me lying on his lower legs. Eventually he calmed and could be released. The next day he approached me, offered his hand to me, and with tears in his eyes, apologized. That stirred me inside. He really *did* care; he really *was* aware there was a broader view.

I work with Jerry to this very day, years after I participated in that takedown, and we work on articulation and defining words. He can be a delight to work with, although again, he's not the "type" I had pictured myself with. He has impressed me with his ability to define words such as *solar*, *aviation*, and *physician*. I felt for him recently one day though, when he appeared agitated and out of sorts. As it turned out, he told me that Mother's Day had been a difficult day for him and that Father's Day would be hard as well.

Jerry still speaks using incorrect pronouns. I'd come to terms with the fact that there are some things in life that will never change, that he would never use pronouns correctly, and that it was okay. He completely shocked me about two months ago when he came into the room and stated, "I want to learn how to do pronouns." I was flabbergasted. It had something to do with a conversation he'd had with a house staff. Someone, and God love that person, had finally gotten through. So most recently, we work on pronouns too. I must constantly correct his spontaneous speech when he starts out sentences with "Me was" and "Her is." I stop him in mid-stream and interject, "*I* was" and "*She* is," and he almost always corrects himself on the spot. We do drills every session, and he has taken home index cards with target phrases on them, such as "*They* are" and "Give it to *them*." He tells me he is practicing. May wonders never cease.

Chapter 2

See Jane Run

I first met James about a year after I started with the agency. James was a very young man, in his late teens, muscular and attractive, even after he had completely shaved his head. James came from a broken home and had recently moved from another state to live with his aunt. He had been sexually abused by more than one person since he was two-years-old. James was high-functioning, and from what I saw, well-mannered, though he obviously was street-smart. James was a classified sex offender; he wound up with us because he had seduced a girl of fourteen shortly after his move.

James had a repaired cleft lip and palate, though there was very little evidence of that when we first met. He did have a mixed-type hearing loss (mild loss at low frequencies and moderate loss at high frequencies). While with us, James acquired a behind-the-ear hearing aid, though I don't remember him ever wearing it. He also had difficulties hearing speech when background noise was present, and not infrequently had to ask for verbal repeats. (James demonstrated signs of central auditory processing disorder, or CAPD.)

James loved country music and entertained thoughts of playing both piano and guitar. The male staff saw right through his perceived machoism and made it clear they did not care for him. (I heard more than one male staff member state, "I don't like him at all.") During his first appearance in the agency's yearly talent show, he had played an electric guitar solo, trying to make himself out as a real sex god. He had stripped down to a skimpy T-shirt and had attempted a heavy metal "riff."

James was placed in the same IEP class as Jerry, which was for those under the age of twenty-one. When I first started seeing him, our chief psychologist expressed concern about the two of us being alone in a room. He believed that James was sure to accost a woman during his stay. As with all my students, I made sure the door was always propped open and I never had any troubles.

We worked on many things over the next three years, including reading, looking up information, practicing querying via phone calls, geography, and simple math. We even played Bible Trivia from time-to-time. If anyone had complained about me teaching outside my scope of practice, I would have responded with, "Who will teach it to them if I don't?" There would have been no reply. The time to help was then, and the place to help was there.

James was diagnosed as learning disabled, and not being able to read at his age level was a source of great embarrassment for him. Like so many of the others, he had fallen through the system's cracks. Most of them came from dysfunctional families, and their home lives had been the worst. The "system" didn't know what to do with them. It kept advancing them, while knowing full well they couldn't read. That's why after they committed crimes, people like James ended up with us or in jail. Illiteracy and incarceration always correspond.

James called me "Miss Jessica." He tried in vain to cover up his lack of knowledge and inability to read. If we played a game, and he answered a question incorrectly, he would retort, "That's what I said!" after being given the correct response. (That truly annoyed me.) James's reading choices were made up of novels such as the *Twilight* series and other young adult fantasy books.

The classroom teacher was a man James referred to as "Mr. Ted." To put it quite bluntly, Ted was a short, muscular, overbearing, and downright mean man. He was arrogant and narcissistic as well. Some of his aides were also mean. Ted was always loud and was chauvinistic at times (he had scoffed at my military service, professing unabashedly that he did not approve of "soldiers that were girls"). I think he resented me as a newcomer, moving into the scene and potentially questioning his professionalism, integrity, and educational approach. One day James said to me, "I think Mr. Ted is jealous of you." All I could think was, *Yeah, I'm sure he is.* James was quite perceptive.

Amidst reading, phonemic awareness, simple multiplication, and geography, James spoke to me once about "putting on the armor of God" (Ephesians 6:11, New Testament). I realized then that there was a Christian dimension to him. Despite the temptations that he endured daily, he took in earnest his faith. There were few time constraints in those days, and often James and I would work for an hour-and-a-half at a time. I remember one time when he said, "Next time I want to work for two hours." I had chuckled and told him I thought ninety minutes was fine.

Unlike Charles and Jerry, I felt I might truly be redirecting James's path. Maybe his learning how to set up appointments for haircuts or ordering a pizza over the phone *would* enhance his life. Maybe his reading and math skills *had* improved over the course of time we had worked. That is why I was so disappointed at what happened with his unexpected uprooting and very sudden new scene.

James was moved to a group home about thirty or so minutes away. That in itself wasn't the issue; the problem was the lack of opportunities at his new site. His "vocation" at that point was to clean toilets as part of a larger daily work detail. I cringed when I thought about how much more I could have taught him. It wasn't right. I, however, had no say in the matter. He missed out on forthcoming opportunities and activities on grounds. I could only assume his academics were finished at that point too. He had been cut off from me prematurely and he'd been robbed.

Anyway, I presented James with his first Bible on his departure date. I had written inside the cover that he had been a great student over the preceding three years, and that working with him had been a delight. I remember him then telling me, "You've taught me a lot," to which I then replied, "Go with God." I believe he truly respected me, and I felt genuinely rewarded by that.

In as far as we had been able to go, his story had been a success. I could only hope and pray he would continue to live up to that tale. I respected him too, and I felt almost as if he were my own son. He had really *wanted* to learn. Memories of him will remain with me forever. If only the circumstances of his youth could have been changed.

*****

Everyone on the campus was required to have a yearly communications assessment. I first met Kurt during such a "test." Kurt was tall and slender with shoulder-length blond hair. He always walked slowly, in a simple shuffle of sort. He had been hit by a car when he was on his bike as a kid, and had never been the same. Kurt ended up with traumatic brain injury

(TBI) and a metal plate in his head. He was also diagnosed with asthma, mood disorder, impulse control disorder, schizoaffective disorder, and moderate ID.

Kurt experienced rapid mood changes, a low frustration tolerance, and little control over his rage. (I remember seeing him once as he yelled, "I know my rights!" while staff held him in a takedown on the schoolhouse floor.) He was known for physical assault, and during my tenure had stabbed a workshop peer with a pair of shears. (One of the female staff present had said it was the worst thing she'd ever seen.) He was also known for property destruction, throwing objects, and inappropriate sexual behavior toward female staff (touching, kissing, remarks, etc.). Though not a sex offender, he had been lumped into the sex offender cottage. Appropriate placements were not always the case.

Kurt did have periodic home visits with his family, and I believed he felt relatively close to his mom and dad. During our meeting he had said, "Family is the most important thing" and that they "made him happy." He was pleasant in the one-on-one encounter we had during the assessment. Like the majority in that population, he had little to no relationships with peers. I'm not sure he would have benefited from many of his existing peers in any case.

Kurt was intelligent in a cultured sort of way. He was aware of what was going on around him and understood how the world worked. He made comments about wanting to travel to Hawaii and to other various states. He could converse on a number of things, including classic rock, which really impressed me for sure. He knew a lot about popular music and often made comments and asked questions when he heard the radio, such as, "Who sings that song?"

Again, Kurt had a tendency for angry outbursts. He often turned to profanity and name-calling (he told me during his assessment that he wanted to work harder not to swear). This was typically when he simply did not get his own way. He often pounded the walls. He dominated conversations and his social skills were markedly poor. He would ask the same thing over and over again, such as, "What the hell is your name?"

Kurt did make me smile though. In one of our earliest conversations, I remember him saying that his social worker (who was probably not much older than me) "looked like she was eighty," but that I "looked only sixteen." I thought to myself, *All right!* I'd decided long ago I would take my compliments whenever and from whom I could, albeit a five-year-old kid or a man with a metal plate in his head.

Kurt knew what was going on around him for sure. One time I asked if he would be interested in socializing with James, and he immediately quipped, "Sex offender." That was the end of that.

I was required to recommend some kind of supports for everyone, whether they qualified for speech-language therapy or not. I laugh to this day, because for people like Kurt, I would in writing state, *Staff should engage so-and-so in abstract conversations.* Many of these individuals were smarter than their staff. If some of the staff members tried to have abstract conversations, the individuals would put them into "mind melds" for sure.

Though Kurt didn't officially qualify for speech services, I brought him frequently to my room. This was for his own benefit, and I guess to some degree, for my own. We worked on pragmatic conversation, memory-building, and vocabulary skills. He relished the one-on-one attention, and I got to know him fairly well.

I don't even remember how it came about, but a small Bible study formed on our campus, and I had a pivotal role. Our "minister" was "Chaplain Susan," though she was not an outright clergy. I believe she had a theology master's degree. I was her assistant, and together we planned the lessons. We targeted group and social interactions, speaking, and conversational skills. Often, we had the group do various types of role-play. One week we focused on anger management and rage.

The weekly gatherings were great. Charles, Kurt, and James were among several who attended. I would help them in therapy sessions beforehand to practice readings for the group. During the lessons we would discuss real-life scenarios and how each member of the group would react in such a scene. I believe they all got much out of the entire thing.

One time the group re-enacted the story of the Good Samaritan, with all three playing the lead roles. Kurt actually got on the floor to act as the injured man. Sometimes we all sang songs, and it melted me inside to hear Charles ask, "Can we sing again?"

I suppose the "powers that were" could have taken offense in that we were taking part in religious lessons during official programming time. I'm sure that was some kind of breach. If anyone had confronted us about it, Susan and I were prepared to have responded curtly with, "They're building confidence, learning manners, and wearing ties." Each one attended at his own volition. No one questioned us, as it turned out.

Due to scheduling changes, our group eventually had to disband, which was unfortunate, though what we had done was huge. Chaplain Susan passed away not long after, and I was told that some of the individuals in the Bible study had spoken at the service.

Doing the Bible study gave me a different perspective from the one I had previously held. Even amongst the sex offenders, there was a nature of innocence, of respect, and of actually *wanting* to learn. There really *was* another angle to it. That didn't mean I'd be any less angry if one of them had raped my kid or had even raped me, but I saw things much differently than I ever thought I could. Lest we forget-every story has its sides.

Chapter 3

It's Only a Delusion

Larry is a student whom I've been servicing from the very start of my job. He is in his forties, very tall (maybe even six feet, four inches), thin, with bronze colored skin and black curly hair. All I know about his family is that whatever relatives Larry has are now relocated to another state.

Larry walks slowly, hunched over, with his arms behind his back. He is diagnosed with schizoaffective disorder, psychotic symptomology, and moderate ID. (I was told by a colleague that Larry had once attempted to choke her with a seat belt.) Despite the moderate ID diagnosis, I know for a fact that Larry can read and do simple math, so he's a bit of an enigma.

Larry has an open-mouth posture at rest, and he wears a clothing protector (a more age-appropriate word for a bib) because he frequently drools. His handwriting is no better than a two-year-old's; his letters and numbers are gigantic, run into each other, and are completely unable to be read. But again, he is a mystery. He's amazed me lately with his ability to identify homophones (words that sound alike but are spelled differently and mean two entirely different things). For example, if I say, "Tell me two different meanings for *bury*," he will say, "Strawberry and bury a bone." If I say, "What are two kinds of pair?" he will say, "Pear a food and a pair of pants."

Larry hallucinates often. (From what I have been told, he is fascinated by "seeing" leprechauns.) In sessions, he will suddenly make such statements as, "Shhhh, you're going to wake the baby!" Despite short spurts of talking relevantly, he is prone to speaking to people who are not there. He also uses nonsensical, bizarre, and irrelevant terms. He is known to repeat others' questions as his replies. Reality orientation is part of his behavior plan; for example, a staff member may mention the current date and time or discuss world events while Larry is around. Larry might also be asked questions about his family or peers or be asked about photos and/or memorabilia in his room.

Larry's obsessions are music, stereos, and especially radios. I had a small radio in the speech room on the campus during our early years together. Periodically Larry would confront me, almost accusingly:

"Whose AM/FM Dolby cassette-tape-player radio is that?"

In turn, I would reply lightly, "Larry, it's mine."

Invariably he would shout, "But whose is it Jessica, huh, HUH?"

At that point I would lose my patience and rap my pencil on the table and snap back again with, "It's mine!"

(I rapped my pencil on the table quite often during our sessions.)

Another funny thing that happened long ago with Larry occurred when I showed him picture cards and asked him what he saw on each card. I was targeting his ability to describe each picture with a subject, an action, and an object ("The man is swimming in the pool," etc.). He could do so with no problem. Then one day I decided, just for the sake of it, to hold the cards upside down. Larry paused for a few seconds, stared at the cards, and then came up with the correct descriptions without fail. The fact that the cards were upside down did not faze him. I had to bring it to his attention that the cards weren't right-side-up. How did his mind work?

I especially remember Larry participating in a low-impact exercise group led by Rachael (the OT). This activity was called the "parachute run." The group formed a circle, and each person gripped the end handles of the parachute. In unison, each person would hoist the parachute into the air. One person would then call out a participating peer's name; subsequently the peer would have to let go of the handle and then run to the opposite side before the parachute dropped. If Larry's name was called, he would move his feet painstakingly slow. He would shuffle across like a sloth, with his arms behind his back. By the time he had reached the center, the chute was falling down over his head, and everyone would laugh. Again, there was complete oblivion. (I do remember him asking once, however, when the next exercise group would be.)

Larry was another member of the Bible study, and I remember once when the message had really gotten through. We were talking about jealousy, and Chaplain Susan was asking everyone in the group if they had ever felt envy. Larry immediately spoke up and voiced (while drooling), "When someone else got an AM/FM Dolby cassette-tape-player radio, I was jealous!" He certainly spoke the truth.

Today Larry works on vocabulary and learns to define words such as *capacity*, *dishonest*, *quantity*, and *discount*. He still zones out on me often and will stare into space and laugh. He's proven he's learned the meanings of the various words however, and that's really what it's all about. He continues to obsess on music, stereos, and radios. His response time is still excessive, and no less frustrating overall.

Larry really impressed me recently after he came into the room, and I said, "I like your new glasses, Larry."

No response.

I then said, "What is it called when someone tells you something nice like that?"

Immediately, he responded, "Compliment."

Actually, I was proud of him and also proud of myself. I had really taught him something. *Compliment* is one of his target words. He was having a very good day with communication on that particular day. He named several of his peers in his group home and responded once with "Yes, I saw a movie."

He still makes me laugh. Recently I asked Larry the meaning of *nation*, to which he replied, "Under God."

I repeated with, "But what's a nation?" to which he replied, "Liberty."

Later I asked what the word *beverage* meant. Larry said, "Apple juice."

I said, "But what does the word *beverage* mean?" to which he replied, "Apple cider."

I've tempered myself enough by now so that I no longer rap the table with a pencil, but with a hint of frustration, I asked a final time, "But what does the word *beverage* mean?"

Larry replied, "Kool-Aid." *Gggrrrrr...*

As impressive as Larry's retention can be, sometimes his brain seems completely sealed. He cannot for the life of him retain the fact that Barack Obama was the first black president:

"Larry, who was the first black president?"
"George Washington."
"No, Larry, the first *black* president."
"George Washington."

"Okay, name another president."
"Jimmy."
"Jimmy who?"
"Jimmy Page."
Aye-yi-yi.

Sometimes I suppose he means to get the best of me, though he does it in such a dry, inconspicuous way:

"Larry, how long is a century?"
"A long day."
"No, no."
"All day."
"No, I mean a *century.*"
"Every day."

Another word I've tried to teach him is *invention.* I've tried to impress upon him that the word means something made for the very first time. To date, I've had little success. I've tried to give him examples, such as Thomas Edison inventing the lightbulb and Alexander Graham Bell inventing the phone. Recently was the following:

"Larry, what does it mean to invent something?"
"Lightbulb."
"But what does an inventor *do?*"
"A lot."

ALL THOSE PIECES

"Larry, tell me what an inventor *does.*"

"Make telephones."

"Who invented the telephone?"

"You."

"Larry, who invented the phone?"

"A janitor."

"Please tell me the name of the man who invented the phone."

"Abe Lincoln."

"Come on, Larry, you know this one. Who invented the phone?"

"Jimmy."

"Jimmy who?"

"Jimi Hendrix."

I finally gave up.

Chapter 4

I've Got Your Number

Early on, I became acquainted with a woman named Suzy. She was not one of my students but rather a woman who sat beside me in the dining room at lunch. During the first two years that I was on the campus, a hot lunch was served daily, complete with kitchen and dining room staff. Though the lunch was primarily prepared for the individuals, we as staff members could partake if we modeled appropriate behavior during the meals. I had been assigned a certain class (one of the workshops) to sit with during the meal. In that workshop was Suzy, an early middle-aged woman diagnosed with paranoid schizophrenia, psychotic disorder, and mild ID.

Suzy had been born to a drug-addicted thirteen-year-old mother who had carried out physical abuse. She was very short, probably four-feet ten-inches tall, with very smooth ebony skin. She displayed a big, wide grin at times, with large teeth like the Cheshire cat's. You couldn't be certain as to what her eyes were focusing on, and she always had a glazed-over vacant look on her face. She was known for indiscriminately running out of the workshop and also for having to be physically restrained.

Suzy had some convincing academic skills in reading, writing, and math. The long-term mental damage done to her, however, was very real. Her obsessions were numbers and weights, and she continually perseverated on how many, how high, how many pounds, etc. When she verbally obsessed on numbers, her staff would have to encourage "incompatible activities," such as sucking on lollipops, listening to music with headphones on, and writing down the numbers instead. She was preoccupied with how much weight she could lift, how many repetitions she could do, and so forth. She was the female personification of macho. Her staff had to bolt her bed to the floor (along with her roommate's bed) so that Suzy wouldn't crawl underneath and attempt to do upside-down push-ups against the beds.

Suzy comprehended what occurred around her and what was said to her. Often though, she would give no response when spoken to, or would respond with something unrelated. She generally did not answer questions such as "What did you do over the weekend?" or "What TV shows do you like?" Instead, she would take opportunities to engage others in the topic of her exaggerated physical strength, or anything related to numbers themselves. (My supports recommendations stated that staff should encourage

Suzy to use language socially and appropriately when possible, and to verbalize relevant ideas.)

Suzy talked using complete sentences and used language to convey her thoughts. Her speaking skills were superb. She was known, however, to hold "group" conversations with herself, in which she took on the identities of two or three different people, speaking in completely separate roles.

I had to laugh the first time Suzy told me that she could lift "infinity times fifty." I asked her if she knew what *infinity* meant, and she surprised me by without hesitation replying, "It means it has no end." Her comments at lunch amused *me* to no end (with no intended pun!). For instance, here are some of her statements with a few of my own interjections:

"I was the strongest baby in the world. I did headstands and handstands in the Mississippi River."

"Jessica, do you think you or me or anyone else in this room can do anything infinity times?"
"No, Suzy."
"Well, I can."

"Jessica, how many people do you think I can bounce off my knee?"

"Jessica, how much is eight-hundred pounds? How much is eight-hundred pounds?" (After one of our male food servers spoke of a cycle weighing "eight-hundred pounds.")

"Well, Suzy, I have to tell you, an eight-hundred pound motorcycle *is* eight-hundred pounds!"

"Infinity, infinity, infinity," Suzy whispered under her breath. (I had innocently made the mistake of mentioning "Club Infinity," a local establishment, to the male food server, while Suzy listened in).

"It's hard for me to not talk about numbers, Jessica. Why can't I talk about numbers all the time?"

"When I get outta here, I'm gonna be a boxer, 'cause I'm strong!"
"Oh, really, a woman boxer?"
"Mohammad Ali's daughter knows how to box!!"

And there were times when she truly monitored her own preoccupation:

"Suzy, how was bowling yesterday at the plaza?"
"Good."
"What score did you get?"
"I can't tell you."
"Why can't you tell me?"

"It's not appropriate to say."

"Jessica, I'm not gonna talk about numbers anymore. Starting Sunday, I'm not gonna talk about numbers in here, and not even in my cottage."

"Jessica, I'm not gonna lie anymore. I can lift two pounds ten times for three reps."

As "out of it" as some of our individuals were, I came to realize over time that they had moments in which they were entirely "there." You could be sure Suzy was listening to the conversations of others, based on the questions she asked in return. I also noticed that she showed true empathy for the others around her. When one of her peers told her that he might have to go back to jail, Suzy told him compassionately she hoped that he would not. When Kurt was stung by a bee, Suzy exclaimed (with familiarity in her voice), "Oh, Kurt, I know that hurts." I was impressed with her compassion. How could you not love her? Despite all her deficits and all the strikes against her, there was a true heart of gold at her core.

One day at the end of lunch, one of her staff members tossed out (in jest), "Suzy, do you know how many strawberries were in your bowl?" She just looked at him with that all-too-familiar glaze on her face, as the people in the room began to laugh. I admit *I* was privately amused as well. The staff member was teasing her, realizing that the question he had asked would undoubtably leave her baffled. Literally counting the berries would not be the easiest thing to do. In this case, what was meant as teasing was actually taunting.

On another day at lunch, our version of the "Soup Nazi" told Suzy that she couldn't have a second six-ounce can of juice, and she began to weep. I'd never seen her cry before. The tears were just pouring down as if she'd given up on life as a whole. She wailed, "I just wanna go back to where I came from!" Another one of her male staff members retorted from across the room, "Back to Cottage 97, where the juices freely flow?" She continued wailing, "Back to the hospital…!" As funny as it was, I truly felt sorry for her at that moment. She seemed so utterly helpless and raw. As I would continue to learn, there was a very fine line between what was funny and what was not.

Chapter 5

On the Warpath

I was assaulted in that classroom many years ago, though images from it will remain forever in my mind. To explain, I should tell you that most of us as staff members were trained annually in crisis prevention strategies. These techniques were utilized only when an individual was preparing to or actually hurting himself, herself, or others. Specific to each individual, we became familiar with antecedents to such behavior.

Warning signs could range from things as simple as laughing, staring, pacing, withdrawal, restlessness, and lack of affect. Signs could also be more alarming behaviors such as crying and screaming. Ideally, crises could be averted through such proactive strategies as active listening, distraction, redirecting, reassurance, understanding, and/or humor. Other proactive strategies included relocating to a quiet place, placing a physical barrier between the person and his target, light physical touching, planning to ignore, and/or allowing the person to vent.

"Living to tell the tale," however, was always paramount, and when proactive strategies failed, strategies of crisis intervention (SCIP) were used. The least restrictive strategies were of course, the more ideal. We learned what we needed to know, however, and utilized techniques as each situation required.

Some of the many strategies were: one- and two-person escorts, front hair pull release, bite release, back choke release, standing wrap/removal, arm control, arm release, and two- to four-person takedowns. (You may recall that I took part in a four-person takedown on my student Jerry.) Another one of the techniques is called deflection, which is precisely what I relied on when Terri came charging at me. I had just enough time to put my arm up and shield my face when the attack occurred.

Terri was a middle-aged woman, quite unpleasant and very unattractive. She was antisocial, kept to herself, and when she did speak, it was in a cackling pitch. I had merely walked into that room, but something about me had triggered some primitive "fight or flight" response. She chose the former. It all happened so quickly that it was difficult to react other than shielding my head. I don't remember any pain.

Other staff familiar with Terri said that they were really surprised by the attack. Anyway, when all was said and done, and after that female staff had fortunately come to my rescue, I started out by placing an ice pack on my wound. Because it was a human bite (more potentially dangerous than any animal bite) I would later have to go for a tetanus shot. The "powers that be" were permitted to tell me that Terri was hepatitis-free but could not reveal her HIV status. (No worry, Terri was surely "carnal knowledge-free.")

I wondered if the psychiatrists had readjusted her medications (as they often did with our individuals) and if that was what set her off to start. To this day, I'm nervous around her and try hard not to let her eyes meet mine. Honestly though, the scar on my arm was in some way a badge of honor, and I retained it for several years.

The only other time that a person attempted to assault me was at the dining room table at lunch. As I mentioned previously, there was a particular class to which I was assigned to join (Suzy having been one from that class). The class included an older man named Edmund, who had schizophrenia, OCD, intermittent explosive disorder (and how explosive he was!) and mild ID. Edmund was verbal but most often very quiet. He relished it when I on many days broke up pieces of candy bar to offer him, but he was nonetheless a Jekyll and Hyde. One minute he was the sweetest old man you could imagine, and then the next minute he was full of fury and wrath.

Though not large in stature and certainly far from young, Edmund was surprisingly strong. He was known to do considerable harm to others, whether they had provoked him or not. One day when I was sitting right beside him, that animal rage, just like Terri's rage, appeared in his eyes, and I knew he was going to attack. He leapt up just as I also jumped up and circled around to the other side of the table. James, who was seated nearby, jumped up and tried to intervene while another female staff screamed at him to sit back down. I don't remember exactly what happened, but for some reason (God's grace), Edmund backed off. I remember a male staff approaching the table and stating, "He's not going to do anything." Most fortunately, I came out of that one unscathed. It could have ended much differently.

Later James told me, "They laughed at you for moving around the table, but I thought you handled yourself well." ("They" included the female staff that had shouted at him to leave the situation alone.) I really felt hurt by hearing that. One of the SCIP strategies calls for "putting an object in between the attacker and you." That is exactly what I had done. Was I supposed to just let him tear me apart?

A short time later, I was at a meeting concerning Edmund as a whole. The daytime manager from his living unit said that the only thing really to do when he attacked was to simply "get away from him." So then, what I had done was the right thing after all. I also took note that it was primarily James who sensed the urgency of my situation. He truly came to my aid in time of need and I never, ever forgot that. He was willing to take the blow for me if that's what it ultimately came to.

Not frequently, but sometimes, individuals physically assaulted their own peers. I remember once when a young man physically assaulted a young woman in their unit (the unit was one of the lockdowns). The young man could hear but was nonverbal and was able to use some ASL (American Sign Language). I went along to help interpret when he went before a judge. The judge was to determine if the young man could even be declared competent to stand a future trial. After two different competency evaluations, in the end, the young man was deemed unfit to do so.

Unfortunately, attacks on staff were common (that fact added to the enormous strain placed on our direct care staff). One of my peers, a social worker named Beverly, told me of an incident she'd had with a female "client." Beverly and the other woman were sitting opposite one another at a table. The woman had reached over the table, grabbed Beverly's long hair tightly with both hands, and refused to let go. Beverly had to knock the table over to obtain release.

Another one of my colleagues did not end up as fortunate as Beverly and I had after being attacked. Margie was a psychologist who worked closely with an extremely emotionally disturbed young woman named Ann. Ann had been traumatized after years of physical abuse as a kid. Unfortunately, Margie believed that over time the two of them had built up a relationship that was both credible and solid. She believed that Ann really trusted her, and she also trusted Ann.

One day Margie took Ann through one of our isolated, enclosed walkways (which had been built for passage during extremely cold weather days). Keys were needed to both enter and exit the walkway. Ann turned on Margie and began beating her senseless in the tunnel. Margie, on the floor, tried to shield her face, and therefore her arms took the worst of the battery. She said that she'd managed finally to jump to her feet and began to "scream like a maniac." Ann had fled (only to be apprehended by a male staff who happened to hear the commotion). The way Margie described it later, Ann had admitted that she'd waited for a time like this to attack, kill Margie, steal her keys, and finally escape. When I saw Margie a full week after the attack, one of her arms was still solid blue, badly bruised from the beating. She attempted to press charges, but from what I understand, Ann was another one deemed incompetent for trial. Though Margie fully recovered and resumed her normal life, complete justice in this world was not to be.

Chapter 6

Hear No Evil, Speak No Evil

One of my students in the early years was a completely deaf man named Karl. He was deaf because his mother had contracted rubella during her pregnancy with him. Karl was young when I first met him (in his twenties), and he was of medium height and build, attractive, with auburn-colored hair.

His case was another very sad one, I'm afraid. Through a court order, he'd been placed onto our site. The "nuts and bolts" of his story involved him being accused of sexually molesting a young boy. Because of his deafness and lack of standard communication skills, the courts hadn't known how to proceed. He had not been given the opportunity for an actual trial stand.

Karl was fluent in ASL, and unfortunately I was not. Karl's was a case I had inherited from another SLP who *was* fluent in ASL. I did the best I could with him and tried to communicate with him in sign. He actually helped *me* better learn how to sign. He also had some rudimentary English writing skills.

To be honest, this was so very long ago that I don't remember all of what we focused on. I do remember working on reading and comprehending English print.

After readings, I would have him answer questions, both fill-in-the-blank and multiple choice. I remember being somewhat impressed that Karl progressed with his language skills more quickly than I had foreseen.

I also remember writing up a really cool *Lord of the Rings* quiz for him, because I knew he loved the movies. That was fun. I wish I could say that about our whole experience, because it wasn't fun. There was a time in which he tried to write out a "statement" for me in very rough English print. The gist of what he tried to express was that he was "very sorry" about what had happened with the young boy, but that he really hadn't done it. What was I supposed to say or do?

Karl's case seemed to be permanently stalled; he could not stand trial, but he could not leave our system either. He worked in a prevocational workshop converting medical records onto microfiche, and his frustration mounted to what level I can only imagine. He was so young, and his disability was certainly no fault of his own.

Sometime later Karl moved to a different group home in our system. The last I heard he had taken up Nazi "Sieg Heil" salutes and been assigned to yet another more secure facility. His story was not a winner. I felt that my experience with him had been anticlimactic, had gone nowhere, and was not a success.

Don was another individual and, like several of the others, came to us at the age of twenty-one. I don't think it was a matter of aging-out of his then placement, but rather the fact that he'd become too aggressive for the setting itself. The discontinuation of his thioridazine medication had led to parasuicidal gestures, property destruction, and leave without consent. Don was an intended miracle as he was to be "cured" at our site and then returned after ninety days. (Right.)

Don was diagnosed with profound deafness, moderate ID, ASD, OCD, attention deficit hyperactivity disorder (ADHD), and osteopenia. He also had a history of petit mal seizures and SIB. He had attended a school for the deaf until the age of eleven, then moved to a treatment facility designed specifically for the hearing impaired.

Don knew quite a bit of functional ASL. His parents were both deceased, but he maintained ties with a local support group for the deaf. On Sundays he attended church services designed specifically for those who were hearing impaired. Don really enjoyed the times he was able to spend with others who happened to be deaf or hard-of-hearing. He often went out to Sunday lunch with those he worshipped with at the church.

Don's ongoing obsessions involved such things as gutters, lights, and pipes. He lived in order to plug in and unplug lights, overloading the circuits when he plugged so many in at once. This happened most frequently at

Christmastime, although it also occurred throughout the year.

Don also loved to "play" right outside his group home, tearing off the gutters after he'd filled them with debris. He would continually beg in sign language to be able to go to the *orange store* (undoubtedly Home Depot). I don't know how staff dealt with all of this. Don would go from person to person, trying to explain his intentions for the lights and gutters and pipes through sign. His behavior plan mentioned the need to validate the "coolness" of his ideas, but of course, this validation had its limits. And yes, Don did respond violently to many staff members who attempted to minimize the value of his escapades.

Don suffered in multiple ways. He loved to tease his peers but unfortunately could not endure being teased in return. His deafness itself left him communicatively isolated, as few staff members in his home knew how to sign. That left Don understandably distraught. In general, by the time a staff member learned enough sign to communicate with him, he or she would inevitably transfer to a different home. The combination of his deafness and his behavior was usually enough to frighten employees away. New staff would come in (people who knew no sign), and the vicious circle ensued.

The Sundays spent in the deaf community were positively reinforcing for Don, but inevitably he had to return to the home on Sunday afternoons. Unfortunately, this meant that he returned to his often-disconnected world. He did have a signing psychologist who visited and communicated with him every week, giving him a chance to fully air his grievances in a manner of being "heard."

There was a nearby city that had several deaf group homes, but Don remained far too aggressive to be considered for any of them. He often pleaded (in sign) to be sent to jail and signed *jail*, *cops*, and *hospital* often. No all-out physical takedowns were allowed due to Don's osteopenia, but some of the various other techniques were approved for the times in which he needed restraint.

I had attempted speech therapy services with Don, but we couldn't get beyond his obsession over the coffee maker in the speech room. "Therapy" was a complete fiasco. I did remain involved for some years though, training staff in Don's house in basic ASL. Don would even participate in those classes at times. He did have his docile and pleasant side. He would smile throughout the classes, as he appreciated the overall effort of others to learn to sign.

Sometimes Don would be on the front porch when I drove by the house (no doubt masterminding one of his projects), and he would usually wave to me. I always recognized him by the colorful baseball caps he wore. I installed a shaker alarm system with a flashing strobe light in his bedroom to alert him in case of fire. I had to prompt him to keep the shaker probe under his pillow (he had wanted to put it under his mattress instead).

Unfortunately, Don's passions rarely led to any finished product that you or I might find fulfillment from. Don's OCD was very difficult to manage, in that staff rarely knew what were his ultimate goals. Antecedents to violent behavior usually involved Don being thwarted in his grand compulsive plans. He was completely miserable within the campus classroom setting. Eventually he was switched to an off-campus workshop where I think he fared a little better, at least at the start anyway.

At one point, Don was able to have a Sorensen Communication Service installed in the home. This involved a device that enabled him to make phone calls through his TV. When he called someone (who also had to have the device), the two of them could see each other on the screen while communicating in sign. The service also provided a translator. If Don wished to "talk" to a non-signer, he could contact an operator who would translate Don's signs into speech for the person at the other end, and vice-versa. I remember setting up a few conversations through the Sorensen between Don and his deaf and hard-of-hearing friends. Sadly though, there were times that he became so enraged at the moment's issue that he would break his own device. Repairs were time consuming as well as costly.

Don suffered from the lack of a significant two-way relationship with a female peer. Soon after his arrival to us, a very high-functioning young woman came to live at our site. There were indications of a possible friendship or even a romance with her. (This particular woman happened to be the only individual I knew of on the site that had been officially deemed able to sexually consent.) From what I understand, this woman had "led him on" and then abruptly lost interest after she'd met the "bad boys" (namely, the sex and law offenders).

Some years later, Don became close to a female housemate. They really seemed to click for months, and it appeared that Don had finally found some joy. I remember attending his bowling banquet; the two of them were together at a table, and his face absolutely glowed. Sometime after that, the housemate relocated to a different town. After she and Don started regular visitations, I believe his intensity started to grate on her nerves. She became disinterested and emotionally disengaged. He did not deal with the rejection well (who would?). He would often walk from staff member to staff member, signing the letters of the woman's first name. I saw him once after she'd rejected a greeting card that he'd chosen especially for her. Tears were running down his face and a female staff was trying to provide some assurance. Some months later, however, I saw him again in the group home, and he appeared to be back to his "norm." Though it had taken weeks and weeks, he had finally let it go.

Chapter 7

The Gang's All Here

One of the most touching individuals whom I serviced over the years was a middle-aged man named Barry. Barry was a loving and passionate person, but had unfortunately harbored a death wish. He was bright, personable, and wickedly funny. He was also very intuitive and knew how to use slang. Barry, however, had suffered from extreme depression over the entire course of his life.

Because of his suicidal tendencies, Barry ended up in the pica unit on grounds. The term *pica* was one that our agency loosely used. Technically, it refers to people who ingest inedible objects that they recognize as things to eat. Our pica individuals swallowed items for the sole purpose of self-harm. Just as there was a special unit for sex offenders, we had a special lockdown unit for "pica people." (I had to be cautious and not use handheld glass mirrors with my pica students in speech. You can imagine what self-injury could be done with pieces of broken glass.)

Most of Barry's unit consisted of individuals who needed one-on-one direct support staff around the clock. This included while sleeping, showering, and toileting. No ingestible object could be loose where Barry was near. As he had a history of swallowing items (such as batteries, broken pieces of plastic, etc.), his bedroom was stripped completely bare.

Barry had a "happy light" in the winter to help treat his seasonal affective disorder (SAD). I knew that Barry felt emotional ties to his family. I remember when his mother was ill, he spoke with his dad on the phone, gently asking, "How is Mom?" Despite all his problems, and all that he must have had weighing on his mind, he was still truly concerned about his folks.

When I had first met and assessed Barry, I discovered how warm and witty he was. He told me his favorite band was Guns N' Roses, and then he named a few of their songs. He also stated that he liked to listen to Elvis Presley. After the evaluation was over (and I had determined that he did not need speech services), he started singing Carol Burnett's, "I'm so glad we had this time together…" closing theme song, making me truly laugh.

Though he didn't officially qualify for services, I had some free time in my schedule. I asked Barry if he would like to work with me on some basic academic skills. He readily agreed to do so. Most of our lessons consisted of short stories about various animals, followed by questions, both fill-in-the-blank and multiple choice. He struggled with all the questions, but never lost interest in the lessons.

Barry's skills were at an approximate level of grade-four. He had tested at an eleven-year-old age-equivalency on the *Peabody Picture Vocabulary Test-Revised (PPVT-R*, a fixture in my field for helping to assess receptive language). I had to be constantly on guard, however, not to bring paper clips or pen caps into his group home when we worked. I even had to be concerned about the staples in the worksheets. Barry really seemed to *like* to learn, however, and he was one of the bright spots in my week.

*****

Group treatments were a big part of campus life. Over the years, I was asked by various social workers and psychologists to co-lead and help facilitate groups, such as dialectical behavior therapy (DBT) and social skills. Several of my students were part of both groups at different times. Social skills group focused on handling relationships, methods of relaxation, how to handle the word *no*, and how to manage stress. "What would you say?" scenarios were often presented; individuals would be encouraged to describe obstacles and how such obstacles might be overcome.

DBT (which I secretly dubbed "diabolical behavior therapy") is a treatment model created to help those with severe emotional and behavioral disorders. It frequently targets those with SIB. The therapy is used to balance validation and acceptance of a person in his present situation with a plan for improving the quality of the individual's life.

My greatest personal success with a group, however, was with my own creation of what I called special group. In special group, I worked along with Rachael, another OT named Amy, and an OT assistant named Claire. We pulled out several of the highest functioning individuals for various lessons once a week. Usually the session began with a lesson and a quiz, followed by a related activity or project.

We observed special occasions, including almost every holiday during the year. The individuals made cards for wounded soldiers on Veterans Day, and I personally delivered them to the VA hospital nearby. We learned about the history of the flag, what each flag fold represented, and all practiced folding an actual flag on the 14th of June.

We learned the history behind Hanukkah and played the dreidel game afterward. Later that year we celebrated Kwanzaa; one of the individuals got to dress in an actual African dashiki. We learned the seven principles, how to place the seven candles in the kinara, and how to place and observe the unity cup. On Mardi Gras we arranged a parade complete with homemade masks and beads. We had matzos and grape juice for Passover/ Holy Thursday and learned how to make crosses out of folded palm reeds. One time we actually built a nine-stage obstacle course in the gym and everyone participated in a timed run.

During election season we learned about the then-candidates and discussed the issues at hand. We built our own ballot boxes, and all "voted," honoring the practice of secrecy. In 2008, we had five votes for Obama and one for McCain.

We went on to study environmental issues, such as destruction of the rain forest and species that were endangered. Some of our individuals actually wrote to Congress to urge action by saving bald eagles. Our students relished not only being able to attend, but also to participate. We never once had a behavioral problem. In retrospect, I knew in my heart that the reason they liked it so much was because we treated them as if they were *normal*. They were worth paying attention to, worth listening to, and worth teaching.

Along with Barry, a young man named Eddie was part of special group. Eddie had entertained me considerably during his initial speech evaluation. He was animated and used hand gestures while he talked. He intrigued me with stories about his ancestors on the *Mayflower*, and about a visit to Sleepy Hollow that was one of his favorite trips.

Eddie spoke in a shrill, high-pitched voice and at an abnormally high volume due to his noticeable hearing loss. His hearing loss was moderate to severe sensorineural (pertaining to both the inner and outer ear).

He exhibited this deficit at all frequencies in both ears. Eddie had hearing aids but refused to wear them, as he'd been taunted by other children for wearing them when he was a kid. His intelligibility was good however, and he attributed that to having had speech therapy in school.

Eddie had a large collection of books and told me he liked Stephen King. His reading and math skills were truly impressive. He informed me he had a strategy for multiplying two-digit numbers in his head. He loved to show off his knowledge, tossing out words like *enigma*, and making such statements as "Looks can be deceiving." Eddie, however, had learning disabilities that were not necessarily perceived. I administered the *PPVT-R*; he scored an age-equivalency of ten years and two months. I must admit that in his own way, Eddie was intimidating. By that, I mean I knew how intelligent he was, and I felt at times as though he could see right through me.

Eddie had frequent meltdowns and often begged to go to the local psychiatric center. He would often urinate in his pajamas while in bed during the night. Later, he would refuse to get up in the morning, lying in his own pool of pee.

Eddie became fond of a young woman in the group named Alice. Alice was tall and thin, with chin-length red hair and some acne. She had a volatile, violent history. As she refused to be evaluated for speech, I had to base my report on notes in her file.

The report described Alice as profane, derogatory, and as one who liked to yell. She apparently had a habit of ignoring others and would put her fingers in her ears and walk away when spoken to. She referred to herself in the third person (as if she were outside her own body), saying, "Alice does this," "Alice does that," instead of "I do this," etc.

Alice understood cause and effect, such as how her lawyer affected her overall life. She could also tell you how her sleeping pills worked and how she could get her staff fired. She liked to walk around singing loudly to music with her earphones in. Alice did not comprehend her father's death and would talk loudly to "Daddy" while staring into the mirror.

Over time, Eddie and Alice became friendly, and Alice seemed to transform into someone very different from the person described in her file. When she was in the group, she was surprisingly cooperative and pleasant. When she smiled, she even appeared wholesome and attractive. She and Eddie liked to talk and hold each other's hands. I remember one instance in which my eyes met hers. She smiled warmly, and it reached and touched me in a visceral sense. I thought of her very differently from that point on. She was human and needed not only to receive, but also to give affirmation.

Sadly, Alice was all-too-soon transferred to a facility providing more intensive treatment, and Eddie was truly crushed. I remember talking with him about it shortly after her departure and him saying "I'm fightin' it," in his high-pitched voice. I honestly felt badly for him. He was hurting, and I was powerless to help.

*****

Several other unique individuals attended special group. One young woman was named Tracy, who was slim with long blonde hair. She had been raised in foster care but was decisively admitted into our agency after stabbing her foster brother with a knife. (Shortly after foster care placement, her original name of "Stacy" had been changed to "Tracy." I can only imagine how her psyche had fared.)

When Tracy was good, she was very, very good, and when she was bad, she truly *was* horrid. She became extremely violent if she did not get her own way. At times, there were no antecedents to her acts. She also made attempts at SIB. She was not supposed to be in the proximity of board games or other items that contained small pieces, as she would try to eat the pieces in order to choke.

Tracy was in the IEP class and received speech and language therapy. Her objectives targeted improvement of her phonemic awareness skills, improvement of her receptive language, and recalling the meanings of words. Like so many of her peers, Tracy experienced tremendous obstacles while trying to learn. She was what she was, and while I welcomed growth, I never expected to be awed. On one occasion, she taught the special group how to make paper flowers, and she made me very proud. She had responded to our mentoring well.

Sally came to us at the age of twenty-one, after aging-out of her then placement in another state. She was considerably overweight, but was nonetheless attractive, on the tall side, with beautiful thick, black hair that she wore in braids. She was diagnosed with anxiety disorder, intermittent explosive disorder, depressive disorder, borderline personality disorder, impulse control disorder, and obesity. All I knew about Sally's childhood was that she had been in foster care after her mother had died. Sally loved to play Pokémon and obsessed over most other video games too. She also liked to watch cartoons.

Food, however, was Sally's passion number one. She continued to find new ways to procure illicit foods, including stealing it from stores. She would sneak food into her room and hoard it, and candy wrappers were sometimes found in her trash. She would also go through cycles of refusing food and then would eat and drink without control. (And when she was too lazy to walk to the toilet, she would roll a shirt into a ball, stand over it, and pee.)

Hitting, kicking, and biting were among Sally's methods of assault. She practiced SIB and would scratch her own hand deeply with her nails. She was also known for property destruction, temper tantrums, and verbal abuse. Periodically, it was necessary for an all-out four-person restraint.

Sally worked in one of our workshops; overall, she did not fare well. She would scream, "I don't want to be with retards!" while pulling off her clothing and urinating on the floor. On one occasion, she had a meltdown and had to be carried spread-eagle out of the room. During a similar episode, the RN tried to administer sedation. Sally reached up and grabbed the intramuscular needle from the nurse, bending it before she could get the shot.

I worked with Sally for years. She was intelligent and could read at an approximate grade-level-four. (She really enjoyed going to go to the local library and picking out her own books.) She loved learning about dinosaurs, big cats, and science. We also worked on synonyms, homonyms, and articulating the speech sound /r/.

Sally very much needed a mother figure, and she relied on our psychologist Martha to meet her social and emotional needs. If Martha was not available, I was her next best choice. To some degree, she was my very own daughter. She invited me to accompany her to her bowling tournament one year, and it made me feel select.

I hated to see this beautiful woman, so full of potential, continue to exist as a child. At one of her meetings, I had suggested that Sally study for a GED. The team seemed fully supportive of that intention, but the proposal had led to naught. I *so* wanted her to pass that test and have a semblance of a normal life. (I suppose I was too optimistic, and that the idea was not a bit realistic.) Such was her state.

Another one of our group members was named Samuel. I first met him when he was in his late teens in the IEP class. Samuel was African-American, on the shorter side, well defined, and had a shaved head. He was also very soft-spoken. His diagnoses were oppositional defiant disorder, impulse control disorder, childhood trauma, and mild ID. At some point in his childhood he and his brother had been removed from their home and placed into foster care. Though quiet, Samuel could be very aggressive to the point of physical force. Over the course of time, he had carried out multiple violent acts.

I worked with Samuel in speech therapy overall for about three years. Still waters run deep, and I never completely trusted him or was entirely comfortable when he was around. I had to regularly tell him, "Use your words," as he would often say only "Yes" or "No" or use mere head nods or shakes to answer or to reply.

Anyway, Samuel loved to collect sneakers, wanted to "go to Australia," and desired to have a "black Cadillac Escalade with twenty-four-inch rims." He was also another of our individuals who seemed to express himself well through works of art.

Samuel worked well in a small therapy group with Tracy. Some of Samuel's goals targeted auditory processing, pragmatic conversation (topic initiation and maintenance), and social interaction. Another objective involved vocabulary and I tried to teach him relevant words. For a long time, I'd tried to teach him the meaning of the word *courage*. I would stress that having courage meant one was "very brave." He did not seem to be able to recall that at any time. Finally, after two years I asked him if he knew what the word *brave* meant, and he said no, that he did not. That is what I was up against.

Samuel had been chosen to be the king in our special group's Mardi Gras parade. This was problematic, because Samuel had obsessions with both sunglasses and masks. He would frequently have a meltdown if he focused on those things for very long. What the root cause of this was, I did not know. We had to tell him that the king of the parade never wore a mask, but always wore a crown. He complied, and thankfully, we came out of that event okay.

Samuel refused speech therapy once he graduated from the special education class. All I could think was, *what a loss*. After his discontinuation, I heard one day that he had asked staff if anything could take away the blackness of his skin. What a sad reflection of society at large, and what an example of how skewed thinking permeates to the very edge.

Chapter 8

A Different Plane

Nate was a tall student with a crew cut that I serviced for several years. I worked with him mainly to target oral motor skills (he drooled a lot), but to work on simple reading as well. He was a younger man, in his late twenties and early thirties when I saw him for speech. He had been a member of our special group (and incidentally was the man who won the nine-stage obstacle course in fifty-six seconds flat), but truthfully, he was not among my favorites.

I guess I never felt that Nate and I had actually clicked, and he irritated me in a way that's hard to define. (I know that Claire, on the other hand, felt that she and Nate *had* connected, and that he was near and dear to her heart. Apparently, he had overheard her discussing some of her own issues and had provided empathy at a time of real need.) Nate and Charles lived together in a group home for some years; when it was discovered that the two of them had engaged in a sexual act, Nate had to swiftly be moved.

Nate was diagnosed with: severe ID (his full-scale IQ was estimated to be about 46), undifferentiated PTSD, conduct disorder, schizophrenia, and unspecified psychosis. His medications included lorazepam, clozapine, sertraline, olanzapine, and lithium. Nate's childhood had been completely traumatized by abuse (including sexual) and neglect. There was a family history of substance abuse, ID, and developmental delay. His father passed away suddenly when Nate was about fifteen, leaving him more distraught than he probably already was.

After Nate's admission to our agency, he quickly acted out with assaults, fire-setting, defiance, and verbal abuse. He had been hospitalized several times for suicidal and psychotic acts. Nate experienced "auditory command hallucinations," and he struggled with voices telling him to "hurt people" and "kill staff." Several years ago, he planned and executed an assault on a female staff member that had both sexual and retaliatory motivation.

Nate was also known to hurt himself, and there were times he had to wear a helmet to prevent him from banging his head. Personal warning signs included broad-smile staring, clucking and flapping his arms like a chicken, glassy eyes, and performing Jim Carrey's, "The Claw." (He would bend his fingers into a claw-like position and verbally threaten others with, "The claw is going to get you.")

There came a time when Nate began hinting about "wanting to learn to read" every time he was around me. I had my doubts, as I knew in my heart he would never be able to read, and I continued to stall for time. Nevertheless, at his repeated prompting, I finally took him onto my caseload to address his reading skills as well as to help eliminate the drool.

The treatment for the drooling actually worked, and I got compliments from his group home staff telling me they were noticing far less of it at the house. Reading, on the other hand, was a very different case. We spent hours and then days and then weeks and then months on *cat*, *fat*, *rat*, *mat*, etc. Nate could read two-letter words at about eighty percent accuracy, but reading the three-letter simple rhyming words he never could achieve. I did my best and I did a lot of teeth-gritting in those days. Nate hung in there for a few years, but then his attendance eventually dropped to the point in which we both knew it was time to say, "So long and farewell."

At the present time, Nate works in a vocational service setting, and describes his dream job as one in which he could "wash people's cars." I understand that he is close to his aunt and to his grandfather, who is in declining health. Anyway, he speaks on the phone with his grandad quite a bit. Nate is his own advocate, having no official guardian. A former staff member serves as Nate's volunteer, and he goes to her home for holidays and occasional visits.

Nate enjoys watching football, playing basketball, and playing cards (he loves to play a simple card game he says he invented called "trash," and he taught me once how to play). Nate also loves video games, though playing too many of those, especially in the middle of the night, increases his psychotic thoughts. Nate enjoys earning outings for his good behavior, and all things considered, I believe he is doing the best that he can.

*****

There were individuals whom I did not personally service but who still left impressions on me; some of them I would like to describe. Todd was a high-functioning, autistic man in his mid-sixties with grey hair and glasses. His official diagnoses were atypical ASD, impulse control disorder, OCD, and mild ID.

Todd was employed in a vocational workshop where he was described as "a very proud employee." His obsession was with the Beatles. He could be heard muttering "Yellow Submarine" and "Ringo" frequently under his breath and could name all the Beatles' albums that were ever made. Todd was also fixated on food and was in constant anticipation that he might miss a meal. He was another who referred to himself in the third person ("He's going to eat dinner tonight" or "Todd gets to eat, right?").

Todd would physically grab a person to gain the attention he craved. He would also talk to himself and echo what others had said. He stated his birth date often (including the year) and would ask others about their dates of birth. Todd would frequently ask me, "Are you staying for dinner tonight?"

Todd had positive relationships with his immediate family, especially with his mom. He would name his mother's home address often, and he would even go for out-of-state trips to visit his dad.

Todd exhibited no eye contact that I ever saw. (When I had assessed him for communications, I suggested that staff encourage him to use eye gaze and to refrain from cutting off others' speech in mid-stream.) He also had no gag reflex. I had seen him swallow whole baby carrots and three-inch celery sticks in *literally* all of two seconds, without any signs of distress. Needless to say, the IFEAST team had downgraded his diet to one-inch pieces cut-to-size. Recommended dining techniques included staff presenting Todd with only a few bites of food on his plate at once, the use of youth utensils, and Todd placing his fork or spoon down between bites.

Another member of Todd's household was Marianne. One of our most psychologically disturbed individuals, Marianne was possibly the most disturbed of them all. One of our social workers said that she sympathized with Marianne more than with any other, and described her as "an extremely tortured soul."

Marianne was diagnosed with psychiatric disorder, schizoaffective disorder, autism, bilateral hearing loss, and mild ID. She was also blind in one eye. Medications she was on included: olanzapine, metoprolol, darifenacin, seasonique, ziprasidone, zonisamide, pentosan, metoclopramide, and lorazepam.

Marianne was required to have a one-on-one aide with her at all times. She wore a helmet for self-protection and was very prone to physical assault. Her expressions rarely, if ever, appeared as what we understand as "normal." Her eye contact was intense at all times, and she appeared to be constantly in some sort of distress. Violent episodes occurred not infrequently, most often directed toward staff.

A Caucasian woman, Marianne was obsessed with wanting to be black. She had dyed her long, stringy, carrot-colored hair to a jet-black, and her all-time favorite song was Patti Labelle's, "Lady Marmalade." She was not in need of speech or language therapy, but when I assessed her, she wanted to know when I was going to teach her to talk like she was black. She made bizarre statements such as "I'm gonna dip him in a chocolate vat." During my assessment, she told me her favorite band was "Meatloaf" (not bad taste, with no intended pun!). I'd recommended that staff help Marianne determine fact from fiction and the absurd.

Marianne was overly interested in strange people and would make such comments as, "You're cute," or try to stroke or kiss others' hair. She was part of a workshop, but she didn't do much apart from sleeping, slouched over a large desk. She generally avoided tasks and often avoided meals.

Reliability from Marianne's audiology test was poor (she had fallen asleep during the audiologist's evaluation, after stating that she was "ignoring the entire thing"). The IFEAST team had seen Marianne several years ago, after she'd reported having things "stuck in her throat." It turns out the sticking in her throat was related to forced emesis (vomiting), and she was obsessed with throwing up. She also had to be carefully guarded, as she would do such things as use the toilet to get a drink.

I saw Marianne recently, when my fiancé Nick and I visited one of her peers in their group home. As soon as we entered, she ran up to us quickly. I said, "Hey, Marianne, how's it going?" while reaching out and touching her arm. She gave no reply and no response other than her usual glazed-over look. She then went up to Nick, resting her chin on his shoulder, until a staff member pulled her away. She was showing affection in the only manner she knew.

I must say that I was at a complete loss when it came to people like Marianne. To say that I was uncomfortable around her was absolutely true. She was completely unpredictable, and I never knew how to react. She was so disturbed that it disturbed *me* to have her near me, and I didn't know how to deal with such distress. I continued to know the boundaries of my own comfort zone.

Chapter 9

The Show Must Go On

One of the most memorable experiences in my career was the agency's final talent show. The show took place on the campus, and I acted as "Masterette of Ceremonies." I had merely attended a few previous such shows on grounds, but this time around I wanted an actual role. Firstly, I wanted the challenge of serving as MC because I've never felt comfortable speaking in front of people in large groups. More importantly, I wanted to encourage at least one of my students to participate and to also serve as a coach for those who did.

I'll never forget the first show planning meeting that was held. Several of my students and other favorites were there, including Nate, Jerry, James, Barry, Suzy, and Kurt. After several ideas for a possible theme were offered, a vote was taken, and the theme of "The Four Seasons" was selected. Next came the question as to how much staff help would be required. Specifically, it was questioned as to whether various living unit staff should be petitioned to help. I had to laugh when Kurt piped up, "Don't let them help! They're dumber than dirt!"

Kurt was funny all right, so funny that I proposed that he and I do some stand-up comedy jokes in the show. As MC, I needed a multitude of "filler" lines of my own. I purchased a jokebook and came up with what I thought were both appropriate and amusing jokes. Anyway, each individual participant was assigned a staff member to work with and to receive help with his or her own act. (And yes, some of the living unit staff were tasked!)

The show was held on a stage in the gymnasium of the school. One of the classrooms with lower-functioning individuals opened with a flag ceremony and the Pledge. James had an early act; he had "composed" a New Age piece of music for the piano. He played some of the piece while standing with his frontside facing the audience, while reaching backward for the keys. This was a sort of Jerry Lee Lewis–type antic. He was pleased with his performance, and his appearance was certainly more professional than when he'd done his sex-god guitar solo for the previous show.

I was nervous throughout the whole presentation but tried not to let it show. As funny as I thought my jokes were, not that much laughter ensued. I remember telling the crowd, "You can start laughing any time now." Keep in mind, all jokes had to be of the simple and tasteful kind. I'll tell you some of the jokes and let you be the judge:

"Hey, did you ever hear the rope joke? Oh, just skip it!"

"Did you hear about the boy who put his grandmother's dentures under his pillow?
The tooth fairy left him a fake ten-dollar bill!"

"What did the lion say to his friends before the hunt?
Let us prey!"

Or how about these restaurant jokes:

"Did you hear about the restaurant on the moon? Great food, but no atmosphere."

"One customer says 'Waiter, what's this insect in my soup?'
The waiter says, 'I don't know, I'm a waiter, not an entomologist!'"

"A second customer says 'Waiter, there's a spider on my food!'
The waiter says, 'I'm sorry, sir, we don't allow pets in here!'"

Or these "Most Lousy Excuses for Forgetting to Have Your Homework Done":

"You told your teacher your furnace stopped working so you needed to burn it for fuel."

"You told your teacher you didn't realize it was due January 10th of *this* year."

"You had to use it for toilet paper when your plane went down in a field."

"You told your teacher it was confiscated for national security reasons and you can't say any more."

"You said your agent won't allow you to turn in your homework until the movie deal is done."

"Your parents couldn't finish it, so they took it to work to get some help!"

Well, I thought the jokes were funny anyway.

Kurt and I were the fifth act titled "The Doctor Is In!" Kurt played the doctor, and I played the patient. Here are some of our lines:

"Doctor, you have to help me out!"
"Which way did you come in?"

"Doctor, everyone thinks I'm a liar!"

ALL THOSE PIECES

"That's really hard to believe!"

"Doctor, I broke my arm in two places!"
"Don't go back to those places!"

"Doctor, can you get this quarter out of my ear?"
"My goodness, why didn't you come before?"
"I didn't need the money until now!"

"Doctor, I feel as sick as a dog!"
"Then maybe you should see a vet!"

"Doctor, I think I need glasses!"
"You sure do. This is a barber shop!"

"Doctor, I think I have a split personality!"
"Then you'll have to pay twice!"

"Doctor, what should I do if my ear rings?"
"Answer it!"

"Doctor, what did the x-ray show of my head?"
"Absolutely nothing!"

"Doctor, what news do you have for me?"
"I have some bad news and some worse news."
"Give me the bad news first."
"You've got two days to live."

"Heavens, what could be worse than that?"
"I've been trying to call you since yesterday!"

Kurt generally forgot the punch lines; I had to whisper them quickly enough for his response while keeping the presentation alive. He seemed to really enjoy performing, and I had an absolute ball with our act. I was truly proud of us both.

Most of the acts were singing and/or dancing routines. Larry sang "Happy Birthday" a cappella, drooling all the way. Nate sang Bobby McFerrin's, "Don't Worry Be Happy." There was an Elvis impersonator, while others sang and danced to Sonny and Cher's, "I Got You Babe," Nancy Sinatra's, "These Boots Are Made for Walkin'," and the Captain and Tennille's, "Love Will Keep Us Together."

Suzy stole the show with a "Bobby and the Chiclets" act; this was a Motown gig. Suzy dressed to the teeth in a glittering pink 1960's dress while donning a big black poofy wig. Meanwhile, her group sang to, "Stop in the Name of Love!" She was truly a hoot. "Bobby" also came back to sing to Bill Haley's, "Rock Around the Clock."

Terri (*grrrrr...*) sang to the Beatles', "Ticket to Ride" (I was not impressed). Jerry showed his talent by singing and dancing to Billy Ray Cyrus's, "Achy Breaky Heart." He did the splits during the act, and boy, could he dance!

Barry burned Mr. Ted in a personal joke act, which I found an absolute delight:

"Mr. Ted is old enough to remember when emojis were called hieroglyphics."

"Mr. Ted has left and right sides to his brain. In the left, there's nothing right, and in the right, there's nothing left."

"Mr. Ted's intelligence is like underwear. It's important to have it, but not necessary to show it off."

You get the idea.

There were other keyboard and drum solos, and everyone came on stage for the finale with Queen's "We are the Champions." All in all, it was a great show, a lot of fun, and an experience that I will never forget.

*****

During the first two years of my job, I described it to others as "fitting me like a glove." I believed I had been placed with so many of the individuals—James, Charles, Kurt, Jerry, and so many more, for very specific purposes. As time went on after the show, I surely lost my zeal. I did not know how it could be reclaimed. Special group was the only thing that kept me motivated and functioning for the next several years. As for the rest, I began to feel there was no real point. I sank into a great depression, and quite truly, I hated my job for what seemed to be an age.

I was so despondent at times that I didn't even bother to clean up my therapy room. What was the point of sorting, putting away, and being neat? What difference did anything make? What was it all about? To add to my dilemma, I was having serious troubles alternating between this job and my job with the National Guard. In addition to my one weekend a month, there were many days during the year in which I had to be at the base. I would go back and forth between the agency and the base often, and my two worlds did not combine. The military's greater message always seemed to be, "You will be perfect!" (Which of course, I could never be.) The people I serviced at the agency were in every way the contrast; in fact, they were fundamentally the most imperfect people in the world.

While I was wallowing in my dysfunction, changes abounded within the system. The time of "de-institutionalization" had arrived for the place I had long ago dubbed as, "lower than a group home, higher than jail."

The campus was to be closed within a two-year period, and all the individuals were to be moved to various group homes within the region. I was then to provide speech services both in the homes and at a local day habilitation facility (better known as a "day hab").

I was adamantly opposed to the changes. I didn't want to be a traveling therapist for one. Secondly, the day hab was an unknown to me and far away from my home. Thirdly, our special group would now have to be disbanded. I had no choice in the matter, however. Seven years after I had started, it was time to move on and out.

Part Two

Out to the Frying Pan

CHAPTER 10

On the Tip of My Tongue

Over the years, there have been a handful of articulation cases, and I've experienced both frustration and joy over those. I've had several students that could not produce some (or any) of the sounds: /k/, /g/, /f/, /v/, /l/, and /th/. It's amazing how many words in the language contain the /k/ and /g/ sounds (*cat, coat, kit, gum, guest, game,* etc.).

I've serviced a young woman for articulation therapy named Patricia for several years. She is in her late twenties, has moderate ID, intermittent explosive disorder, ADHD, seizure disorder, and asthma. Intellectually she is the age equivalency of a two- or three-year old. She is toilet-trained, though she must additionally rely on adult briefs (a more appropriate name for diapers). Patricia is completely ambulatory, typical looking, and heavy.

Though I've never seen it, Patricia reacts very negatively when things don't go as she plans. She is known for tantrums, assaults, property destruction, dropping to the floor, and noncompliance. On the more agreeable side, her favorite pastimes are watching *Dora the*

Explorer and making simple jewelry for others as well as herself.

I first began seeing Patricia for therapy in her house once a week, after she arrived home from her vocational workshop. It was an entirely unsatisfactory setup. Hers was a large group home, and chaos abounded with the many individuals and staff present all at the same time. I found the only half-decent place to do therapy was upstairs in her bedroom, and I had to carry a very heavy wooden chair up the stairs each session in order to have a place to sit. (Incidentally, when I saw Patricia in her house, I had to wait for her in her room by myself several times. It turned out that one of the most dangerous men placed in our system lived in that same house, and he often sought out female staff to assault. The house staff never told me that and let me unknowingly be alone in that upstairs bedroom multiple times. This man would often pop his head in the door and ask me what I was doing there. I'm really fortunate to have come out of those instances unscathed.) In more recent years, I have seen Patricia in our agency's day hab, and staff members drive her in to see me.

Patricia is largely unintelligible to an unfamiliar listener. The sounds that she *can* make are very accurate, but unfortunately, she cannot produce /k/, /g/, or /th/. She also could not produce the /l/ sound when I first met her. We've worked on /l/ for several years now.

With the /l/ in the medial position of a word (example, *hello*), and in the initial sound of a word (example, *light*), she can now correctly produce such words about eighty percent of the time. The remaining twenty percent of the time, she produces words such as *hello* as "heyo," and so forth. She cannot produce the /l/ at the ends of words, and I doubt she will ever have the awareness of this deficit in order to correct it.

When she first came to me, Patricia could not articulate her full first name. If asked her name, she would reply either, "Tricia," or "Patty." After several weeks of working on breaking her name down into three syllables ("Pa-trish-a"), she could finally say, "Patricia."

I worked on /k/ and /g/ (soft palate/velar sounds) with Patricia for a very long time. Sometimes her errors cause me to cringe, such as when certain people respond to a chalkboard scraped by nails. If I ask her, "How are you today?" she replies, "Dood" instead of "Good." Unfortunately, her last name begins with the /k/ sound, and she absolutely butchers the pronunciation of that name, making me grit my teeth. If I have her open her mouth as wide as she can, and then prompt her to make the velar sounds *without* closing her mouth, she can do the /k/ and /g/ sounds in isolation. (In *isolation* simply means making the individual sound itself.) That's it—that's as far as we get with those sounds.

At the end of each session we name items in the room. I run into a shortage of item options when I look around and see a computer, cabinet, clock, carpet, calculator, closet, and so forth. It isn't worth wearing my teeth down to try to have her say those words. The problem is that once an individual has made the same speech errors over the course of twenty-five to thirty years, it becomes deeply engrained. The pattern is then very difficult to change.

What's kept me going with Patricia is her willingness to work hard in the sessions and at least *attempt* to do what I ask of her. Also, staff report that the overall volume of her conversation has increased dramatically at home, and that her speech is now easier to understand. When I am told such things concerning her progress, I feel gently assured that my efforts are not completely in vain.

Now, having just stated that decades-long patterns can rarely be altered, I will tell you about Pete. Pete, who is very verbal, but in the moderate ID category, was in his mid-twenties when I first met him at the day hab. He has also been diagnosed with epilepsy, explosive disorder, and mild cerebral palsy.

Pete has a sweet, gregarious nature when with me, but from what I know, he has often been violent, especially toward staff within his group home. He is the poster child for hyperactivity, despite not being officially diagnosed with such. He is known for hitting, kicking, biting, and pulling hair, as well as inappropriately touching female staff. Pete often swears at staff and threatens to run away to be with family (his siblings are his legal guardians). He is obsessed with monster trucks, hayrides, Halloween, animals that bite, and the "Chucky" doll from the movie series *Child's Play*.

Pete has a marked lisp (his tongue protrudes out of his mouth when he makes the /s/ and /z/ sounds), and he also could not produce /k/, /g/, /f/, /v/, or /l/ when I met him from the start. I have worked with him on both articulation and language skills. I have also worked with him on sequencing pictures for three-step tasks and in determining "which one is different?" within a large photo containing four smaller pics. He performs miserably at both.

We have worked on /k/ and /g/ for an excruciatingly long time, and finally, several years later, Pete has begun to make the /k/ sound in isolation. He can now easily produce a word containing a medial /k/ (such as in *baking*). He went on to producing final /k/ words correctly (such as *back* and *talk*) with truckloads of modeling and cues. He is today making mildly encouraging progress with initial /k/ words (such as *cat*, *cow*, *kite*, etc.) if I model and slowly exaggerate the sound twice, followed by whispering the full word. Most recently his /g/ sound is emerging in this manner too. If I think on it, my eyes well up with tears when I consider his diagnoses, where he's come from, and what he can actually do now.

Pete is today also making enormous strides with answering "wh" (*who, what, where, when*) questions after I read him a three-part sentence ("Bob ate a hamburger at McDonald's," etc.). His /f/ and /v/ sounds, on the other hand, are not emerging, but we really can't ask for the entire world, can we?

Another one of my articulation students was Roberta. In her mid-fifties, Roberta was diagnosed with moderate ID (with congenital rubella), and intermittent explosive disorder. She had a severe bilateral hearing loss, but she did not like to wear her hearing aids (as is the case with so many of our individuals). She was also an insulin-dependent diabetic, needing her blood-sugar level checked several times a day.

Roberta had grey, thinning hair, and was legally blind (meaning her vision was no better than 20/200 in the better eye without correction). She rarely made eye contact (you could never be entirely sure as to what she was focusing on with her pinpoint pupils and striking green irises).

A Caucasian woman, Roberta was obsessed with all things African (her favorite movie was *The Lion King*); if there was any particular reason for that, it was never clear. Staff would entice her to take her medication by stating, "Roberta, it's time for your African Tylenol," and so forth. She was close to her family members, though she very rarely saw them. She also insisted in wrapping up tightly in blankets anytime she was in the house, despite the adequate indoor warmth.

Roberta knew that if she worked successfully with me for the half hour, she would be rewarded with coffee. (I would bring her one of those single packs from hotel rooms, which were both convenient and thoroughly prized. I had purchased some great single packs with fancy tropical packaging when I was in Hawaii—Kona, to be precise.)

Roberta communicated mainly by muttering, and I found her speech irritating and difficult to understand. Of course, her group home staff were accustomed to her and therefore could understand her far better than an unfamiliar listener could. As I recall, Roberta worked on /s/ blend words, meaning the /s/ sound followed by another consonant (*ski, sled, spring, state, scare*, etc.). She did not produce final consonants, such as the /g/ in *dog* or the /t/ in *cat*. I could have modeled those words forever, and she wouldn't have produced them correctly for all the tea in China (or in her case, for all the coffee in Brazil).

Anyway, with Roberta, as with Patricia and Pete, I needed to use a completely behavioral therapeutic approach. I would say a word and then ask her to simply repeat the word immediately after. When Roberta was calm, she would work hard and demonstrate success by producing the words intelligibly. If she became stressed or perturbed, or had started out in a poor mood, she would only scream and cry.

One manner Roberta had of retaliating against me was to speak at such a low-volume whisper that I couldn't make out a bit of what she had said. She would more and more often refuse to participate in sessions. Should I be ashamed to admit that I'd been happy when I called ahead and staff informed me she didn't want to do speech that day? After working with her over the course of two years, she refused to participate nearly every week, and I finally removed her from my roster. Not every battle could be won.

Chapter 11

Matter Over Mind

Wayne was one of my students from some years ago. He was severely hard-of-hearing, with intermittent explosive disorder and mild ID. When I first picked him up on my caseload, I knew little of his story. I did know he'd committed several violent acts against women in his past, including several staff. Some of the outcomes had been severe; at least one of the women was never physically capable of working again. Later I found out that Wayne was known to plot his attacks and isolate his targets, who were usually authority figures who were female. His behavior plan indicated that he should not be left alone with female staff.

Wayne had no contact with any existing family. An older couple acted as volunteer visitors and invited Wayne over to their home for occasional visits. Interestingly enough, one of the female staff members from his cottage was also his legal guardian. I liked him from the start, although I remained cautious at all times when he was near.

Wayne was middle-aged, extremely farsighted, and wore very thick glasses. At the time anyway, he wore one hearing aid, which enabled him to hear only incredibly loud sounds, such as jet engines and fire alarms. His passion and joy stemmed from his job filling vending machines as part of a working team for the agency. He loved the responsibility of the job and made more money than did any of his peers ($10.50 per hour). He could conceptualize the idea of a paycheck and was always proud (outwardly beaming) when he took his check to the bank.

At the time I knew him, Wayne was permitted to walk freely on the campus site, completely on his own. That made me quite apprehensive to say the least, but as he'd had no violent episodes in many years, the "powers that were" deemed it okay. He was observed to show more agitation than aggression in his later years (such as by slamming doors) and had no restrictions of rights (such as by having to keep household sharps locked away). Unable to verbalize, he would vocalize loudly and wave to me if he saw me on the grounds. He also liked to give me and receive back the thumbs-up sign.

I was first asked to work with Wayne at a particularly low point in his life after his pet bird, "Joe," had suddenly passed away. Wayne had some convincing grade-school-level reading and writing skills. At one time he'd had an electronic device called a Dynavox to use to "talk." I'm not sure as to what level he had mastered, but when I first met him, he had no interest in the device. Wayne communicated through gestures, facial expressions, body language, and ASL.

According to the team, Wayne's biggest problem was being unable to express his personal emotions, such as envy and anxiety. (He was then enrolled in an anger management class on the site.) My first strategy in addressing this problem was to have him begin to write down his daily thoughts. (In addition to journaling in speech therapy, I had recommended that Wayne write four additional times a week with the help of his staff.) It was very difficult to relay the purpose and meaning behind the task. He did very poorly overall, looking to me routinely for the answers to what he thought I sought. I decided to seek out another approach.

The next strategy was to present Wayne with pictures of individual faces, each depicting a different emotion. Interestingly, I found that *GQ* magazine contained an abundant source of relevant pics. In traditional magazines, all persons are depicted as either happy or neutral; *GQ* contained numerous pictures of people (men, women, and children) who displayed anger, embarrassment, boredom, surprise, and fear. I would present Wayne with a picture and then teach him the corresponding manual sign. Ideally, he would be shown a picture and would then form the correct corresponding emotion sign. It was very difficult to tell if Wayne was benefiting at all from this teaching, but I went the extra mile with the *GQ* pictures and gave it my very best shot.

My final strategy with Wayne involved devising worksheets containing statements and questions with three to five multiple-choice answers. For instance, I might write,

"When someone gets to go to the mall and I don't get to go, I feel…"

   a. Happy
   b. Sad
   c. Bored
   d. Jealous
   e. Mad

Of course, more than one answer could be applicable or correct. I was never overly optimistic about this last strategy either, and in the end, I never knew how much Wayne really understood. There was one instance, though, that I will never forget. It was holiday time, and the question read, "During Christmas time I feel…"

   a. Happy
   b. Excited
   c. Sad
   d. Mad

We went through the different choices, and Wayne nodded his head "yes" to each and every one. I nodded, mouthing and signing back, "Me too," which was really the honest truth. What flashed through my mind at the time was the difficult time *I* was having with holidays, inevitably the by-product of a series of broken relationships. We were communicating! It showed that not all hope was lost. Our connection had resonated during that moment and was validated all the more when he was the only student to give me a Christmas card that year. That card verified that I was far from forgotten in this world. No matter who *had* forgotten me, this one multiply-impaired man still remembered me. It was times like that, though infrequent, that kept me pressing on.

The following summer after Wayne had given me the Christmas card, I went to see him play softball off the site. This was a special league set up specifically for the developmentally disabled. I was proud to see him participating and interacting with his peers.

I ended up helping Wayne transition from the campus to a group home residence during the period of de-institutionalization. I worked with him on his person-centered plan before the move and tried to discuss his feelings about the changes at hand. This must have helped, because he appeared well adjusted when I eventually saw him at the new house. Though not a triumph, I still considered my experience with

Wayne a success. Reaching a plateau, Wayne decided with me that he be dismissed from speech.

One of my most difficult cases (if not *the* most difficult) was Tom. In his mid-thirties, Tom had a plethora of diagnoses, including: chorea/dystonia (causing an involuntary movement disorder), mild ID, intermittent explosive disorder, impulse control disorder, depression, sialorrhea (drooling), chronic pain (neck, shoulders, head and back), hiatal hernia, gastro esophageal reflux disease (GERD) and constipation. He also was prone to partial seizures and presented with dysfluency (stuttering) in his speech.

Tom was on a host of psychotropic medications, including sertraline, olanzapine, and lorazepam. None of his medications held any power to control the unwanted movements of his limbs. He had received a deep-brain-stimulator implant some several years prior; the implant *did* lead to *some* improvements with the movements as well as with his mood. Tom needed to rely on a wheelchair and wore a helmet during transfers (in the event of a fall). As mentioned, he still had involuntary and unpredictable movements of his legs, arms, and head. He was verbal, though cognitively deficient, and he was unable to read.

Tom lived in a group home with several older "peers" who were in far worse shape cognitively than was he. I believe this setting added to Tom's depression and sense of emotional isolation. He had wanted to live alone or with a younger roommate and had been on waiting lists for such, but was never considered a high enough priority to be moved. Supposedly, all his needs were met at the current group home. Tom had no recent contact with any type of family member, though he had a visiting female volunteer. Tom was very active in self-advocacy groups, and sometimes with the Special Olympics. He attended church, Christian festivals, and described his Christian faith as "something that was very important to him."

    I saw Tom in his group home, usually on Monday evenings after his bus had transported him back from day hab (a program outside of our agency's system). Tom's bus was the latest one possible, as he'd had conflicts with individuals riding the earlier ones. I have to admit that I felt resentment with this entire scene. For one, his house was in the opposite direction of and very far from my own home. I hated getting out of there so late, particularly in winter's darkest months. Also, Tom didn't get home until close to 5:00 p.m. We couldn't begin our session until after he'd eaten his dinner, so I sat and waited in the living room, watching the local news while he dined.

    I first attempted to treat Tom's stuttering. I found out quickly there are no easy cures for such, especially for those with a host of other issues. I tried to educate myself as best as I could on the subject, buying several books and DVDs from *The Stuttering Foundation of America* (SFA).

One of the dysfluency techniques is called "easy onset" or "soft start." This involves the individual gently "sliding" through the first sound of a word. The desired result is a continuity of sound and airflow with no break in voicing and no repeats. A second strategy is called "cancellation," or "post block correction," in which there is a deliberate pause after a stuttered word. Following the pause is an attempt to say the word again while struggling less.

Yet a third technique is called "voluntary stuttering." Just as it sounds, the strategy requires a client to stutter at will. Ideally, the person voluntarily does what he dreads, thereby gaining some self-control over the matter itself. The theory behind this concludes that the client will be given courage and that shame may be reduced. Tom's responses were variable with all three of the techniques. I provided him with a tape recorder so he could listen to himself talk and practice during the week. He never did any of the homework that I assigned. He did try to do the things I asked him to do in sessions, but we were dealing with an uphill fight.

Early on during this attempted treatment, I attended a Christian rock concert with friends in another state. As it turned out, I learned that this particular lead singer happened to be a stutterer himself! A new idea emerged, and I wanted Tom to know he was not alone.

I knew of Tom's Christian background and that he listened to Christian rock and attended related festivals.

I e-mailed the band's fan club, asking if the singer could possibly send an uplifting message to Tom. I also asked if he was touring near our area anytime soon. To my surprise, I got an immediate response from the singer himself! He replied with, "Have Tom send an e-mail to this same address." I was truly excited. I told Tom what had happened, and he was encouraged too. Though I ended up sending three follow-on e-mails on Tom's behalf, we never got another reply. I was disappointed for Tom to say the least. I felt guilty and responsible for building up his hopes which were only to be dashed.

I tried to help Tom in various other ways, such as by ordering a T-shirt for him from the SFA. The shirt had a caption that read: "Stuttering is okay, because what I say is worth a repeat!" I also bought him DVDs that presented stories of stutterers who'd made true headway. On top of that, I read him articles written by those who had struggled with their dysfluency. The truth though, was that the vast majority of stutterers did not have the numerous challenges faced by Tom.

Finally, I attempted to set Tom up with a stuttering support group in a nearby town. I convinced his team leader that Tom would benefit from such a group. She gave her approval for staff overtime to take Tom to the monthly meetings. The first attempt at getting him to a meeting sorely fell through. A staff member was ready to take Tom on a Thursday evening, after having communicated with the woman who ran the group. Bad weather hit that night, and the woman failed to notify the group home that the meeting had been postponed. As you can probably guess, Tom's staff had loaded him into the van and taken him all the way to the meeting site, at least forty-five minutes away. There was only so much I could control, and the entire idea was snuffed out almost before it began. I felt guiltier than ever after the collapse of this second plan.

Shortly after the support group fell through, we decided to switch gears and target Tom's reading skills. This proved to be no easier. Tom knew the individual twenty-six letters but, as with Nate, could not consistently read regular rhyming words, such as *cat*, *fat*, *rat*, etc. Heaven help us when I had presented him with irregular English words (words which in volume of our total language equal one-third!). Tom would ask why such words were put together in manners so very strange. For example, *do*, *go*, *to* and *no* should all in theory rhyme, and yet they clearly don't. Similarly, the words *wood*, *food*, *good*, and *mood* also do not all rhyme. I would have to say, "It's just the way it is. One simply has to know it—there is no rule." I wanted to apologize to him, and I felt guilt all over again. Why does English spelling have to be so absurd? How was an intellectually-disabled man supposed to figure all this out?

I continued to go to the house on Mondays after dinner, but I ran short on new ideas. We both knew Tom was getting nowhere, apart from me providing some basic moral support. The act went on, and there was no hope in sight. One evening very late in the course of treatment, Tom asked me if I thought he was "ready to read a book." What was he thinking? Not so long after that, Tom ended up "firing" me (as other staff had warned me from the beginning that he would do). He decided that he would get his services somewhere else.

One day recently, I saw one of our social workers for lunch. She told me that one of the individuals she serviced had asked her if she would become his ghostwriter. He wanted someone with first-hand knowledge to tell the world what a group home was really like. Not coincidentally, she then told me that this particular person happened to be Tom! Ultimately, I was not surprised. I just felt badly about Tom all around. Looking back at the entire picture, life was just so unfair. All I had to do was waltz in once a week, do my thirty-minute session, and waltz out. Tom was there for the duration of his life, with little hope of much of anything in this world. I asked myself, why did he have to suffer so very much? I could never come up with a reply.

Chapter 12

Tickle Me Pink

Some of the things my students have said over the years have been so very funny. There are students that I had for relatively short periods of time but that I will never forget. I had a student named Dale in the early years. Dale had Down syndrome and was relatively high-functioning. (The only thing I knew about his past was that at one point he had remained in a house on fire until his ears were starting to burn.)

Dale did not enjoy coming to speech-language therapy and would complain routinely with, "This is boring." I don't even remember exactly what we worked on, but he pretended he had a firm handle on whatever was presented. In truth, he had difficulty completing the tasks. He made up tall tales quite often. He told me that he'd walked fifty miles between towns, had been struck by lightning, and that he swam with sharks. When I completed his semiannual progress report, I included those allegations in my write-up. I wasn't at the case review, but the social worker who had run the meeting said that Dale had put his head face down on the table when my portion of the review was read. Apparently, things had backfired; he had ended up embarrassed by nothing less than his very own claims.

Another one of my sweetest and cutest students was named Johnny. Also having Down syndrome (with moderate ID), Johnny stood about four feet, ten inches, even shorter than me. He usually wore tropical-looking Bermuda shorts with matching tops, which made him even cuter than he already was.

Johnny loved coming to therapy and tried very hard in class. I worked with him on vocabulary and correcting his frontal lisp. Additionally, we worked on understanding the calendar (months, days of the week, years, etc.). When there were any extra minutes, we would work on telling the time and math. We were working on simple counting one day, and I asked him, "Do you know what number comes after fifty-nine?" He absolutely beamed while chiming, "Fifty-ten?" I had to smile. I mean, after all, he was right; what is fifty and ten?

For the first few months in the day hab, I worked with a man named Patrick. He was probably about forty years old. Patrick was mentally impaired due to a bout with the chicken pox along with encephalitis (inflammation of the brain tissue) when he was a kid. He had difficulty walking and needed staff to lead and hold him with a gait belt, which unfortunately resembled a leash.

When my location changed and people knew that I would be working with Patrick, they had warned me with, "Be careful, he'll pull your pants down." His records indicated that he had difficulties controlling his libido. How can I explain his presence? He was robotic, always moving in slow motion. His thought processes were incredibly delayed. His speech was painstakingly labored, and he spoke in a complete monotone, such as in, "What…are…we…going…to…do…now…?" He sounded like a synthesized recording that had been dramatically slowed down.

I was at a complete loss with what to do with Patrick. I tried some simple reading but didn't think any approach would benefit him in the end. One time he attempted to close the therapy room door and trap me in there with him. Our day hab director (who was in the next room) heard me loudly shout, "No!" She then quickly ran in, and between the two of us, we got him resituated and seated. All that had flashed through my mind as he jumped up was, "He's got overactive libido, and he'll pull your pants down."

Patrick ended up passing away without warning. Shortly after that, another one of our individuals who was very ill stated he didn't want to die because he "would have to go to heaven and run into Patrick there." (Incidentally, that person actually *did* pass away. I wonder how he and Patrick are getting along today.)

Patrick was one of those students that I had inherited. He was previously seen by my predecessor Ben, who had retired abruptly the same year the campus closed. To be candid, I don't know how Ben could continue to hold on to any joy when coming in to work. Most of the individuals on his caseload were, in my opinion, people *that I* was personally incapable of helping. This job was hard enough servicing those who showed at least a little promise. (For example, one of the women on the inherited caseload made it her mission to routinely urinate in her pants while sitting in the therapy room chair. She gave a big grin every time she did that.)

I will say that I kept almost all the individuals from his caseload for about two years, gradually changing my caseload over to feature those whom I believed I *could* justly serve. And I will also say that despite all my inner resistance to becoming a traveling therapist, I soon found that I really *liked* going to the different houses. I got to engage not only with the individuals but with their staff members too. (I have warm thoughts when I recall the smells of dinner cooking in the homes, while their TVs blared *Wheel of Fortune* and re-runs of *Bonanza*.)

Once I completed a communications assessment in one of the cottages on a young man named Robert. A young man in his early twenties, Robert was diagnosed with mild ID, intermittent explosive disorder, impulse control disorder, OCD, ASD, and seizures. He had gone to school until he was twenty and was very bright, despite only scoring an age-equivalency of nine years on the *PPVT-R*. He could multiply double digits in his head, and he stated that he liked to work and make lots of money. He had many interests including sports and movies (*Hitch* and *Charlie and the Chocolate Factory* being two of them).

Robert's speech was rapid and boisterous, and he often cut my speech off in mid-stream. After he told me that he liked to write poetry and think of rhymes, I asked him to name five words that ended with the letter /k/. He immediately did so, and then turned the tables and demanded that I do the same. I'd never had anyone do anything like that before, and it not only amused me but impressed me too.

I completed another in-the-home assessment on a middle-aged man named Paul. Extremely intelligent, Paul was diagnosed with autism, mild ID, and OCD. He worked in a workshop during the week, packing crates of firewood. He also attended church every week with his mom.

Paul spoke in a whisper-like monotone with very little inflection. He was considered dangerous, as he'd had a history of seeking out little girls with long hair to "tip upside down." I understood this obsession also extended to small-statured adults. Lucky me. (I didn't know the details, but many years ago, he had used his manipulative skills by talking a bus driver into dropping him off at a day-care center for kids.) When out of ear-shot of his staff, he would try to "get away with" asking others if they had daughters, sisters, etc.

Another one of Paul's obsessions was to make "number lists," that is, assigning numbers to staff to decide whom to dress like each day. Paul repeatedly changed clothes if he saw someone he wanted to dress like or realized that the staff's "number had come up." He often wore dirty clothing to give himself more "changing into" choices.

Paul was good at math and could repeat back six numbers in a series forward, and three numbers backward. He spoke in complex sentences and had an excellent vocabulary. I tested him with the *PPVT-R*, and he scored an age-equivalency of twenty-six years. I have to admit, I was impressed that he'd proven his knowledge of the meanings (upon verbal direction, pointing to one picture out of a four-picture choice) of nearly all 175 words (he missed only seventeen). As we progressed to the end of the test, he was showing knowledge of words that even I didn't even have a clue to, such *homunculus*, *calyx*, and *obelisk*. Talk about feeling embarrassed.

For a very short period, when I was still on the campus, I had a man named Brian on my caseload. Brian was very low-functioning with limited verbal skills. His obsessions were foods and beverages, specifically coffee and pop. The first time I saw him I had made sure that my therapy room was void of visible edibles and drinks. When he came into the room, the first thing he did was to grab a *tea bag* that was still in sight and shove it into his mouth! I was stupefied and stood there in disbelief while he chewed and swallowed the bag. I then thought that all was going to be well. I mean, surely, he had realized the error of his way, and surely, he had concluded that the tea bag was not to eat. To my utter dismay, he scarfed down another! This was not what I was expecting, to say the least. Thank heavens the tea bags did not contain caffeine.

Speaking of edibles versus non-edibles, one year on his birthday I gave one of my favorite students named Michael some gifts. (Michael happened to be deaf and communicated through simple gestures and ASL. His older brother and guardian named Darren and I had become good friends over the years, and often took Michael out for treats like pizza and ice cream.) The presents consisted of a bag of ground coffee and a large box of candy. I left these things with Michael after his weekly speech session at his group home. As it turns out, his roommate got into it overnight, dumping it all out on the bedroom floor; he consumed not only the candy, but the coffee grounds as well! Needless to say, his staff were not especially happy that I'd failed to tell them about the gifts.

One assessment I did was absolutely absurd. An older man named Mark, whom I was assigned to see, had a long history of auditory and visual hallucinations and disturbed illogical thoughts. Actually, at that time I was doing both a communications assessment and an IFEAST evaluation. I saw Mark during the dinner meal in his group home late one afternoon. He wouldn't tolerate having me look into his mouth. (Mark was missing nearly all his teeth, and he had refused to have the final teeth removed. His head was down nearly all the time.)

Though Mark's speech was largely irrelevant, at times what was intelligible made perfect sense. When I asked him to eat a particular food, he responded with, "No, I want you to eat it!" He refused to eat during the entire meal, exclaiming, "I'd rather go hungry!" He then stated that he wanted to go to McDonald's. He made such comments as, "You know what I want? I want a beer, a hamburger, French fries, and some cake." When Mark noticed that his milk had been thickened for safety, he accusingly queried, "What's in this milk? I want plain milk!" Finally, he declared, "I want to check and see if my brain is still there. Maybe someone took it!" I decided then and there that Mark did not need help with speech.

One of my very favorites in the day hab today is Peggy. A high-functioning woman, Peggy is now in her mid-sixties and I have been servicing her for over five years. Peggy has schizoaffective disorder and mild ID, as well as some physical stability issues (she walks with a walker). She also has a long-standing history of mood dysregulation, irritability, suspiciousness of others, and paranoia. She is very critical of and competitive with each of her housemates.

Peggy loves to talk (and talk and talk), usually tangentially. She exhibits verbal agitation not infrequently in the home (yelling, threatening, etc.). She also has a history of false accusations of sexual abuse and neglect. Peggy earns puzzle pieces and stickers for good behavior; when she accumulates enough of these tokens, she earns a special outing with staff.

Peggy has three brothers; two of whom live in other states. She has no legal guardian, but one of her brothers acts as her primary advocate. Peggy attends the day hab four days a week, and she has a very small job there folding laundry a few minutes a day. Every other Thursday, she is more than excited when she receives her check.

Peggy is bubbly and a delight for me to work with. Her passions are letter-writing (she reads and comprehends at a second-grade level) and art, at which she excels. She attends sessions twice a week, and we devote most of our time to writing. On her own, she "runs-on" all her sentences, and they make absolutely no grammatical sense. I help with a different letter each and every session; they end up being letters that fortunately *do* make sense.

Peggy writes to family members, staff members, and friends (she impresses me with how she has all their addresses memorized, including the nine-digit zip codes). She loves to write to her three brothers, and she inevitably begins her letters as with, "Dear Mr. Brother

John Raymond T…" She is incredibly funny, and she is dead serious about the things she is funny about. For example, she will ask her brother, "How is your bed partner today?" Despite my objections, this is entirely valid wording in her mind, and is usually what ends up in a typical note. These are examples of Peggy's independent writing (actually, the first example is some of her better writing):

> *Dear Mr. Brother Liam Edward T.,*
> *I am wishing you can come today to my state. I like you today call me on the telephone. See if my brother Mr. Robert George T. can send me stamps? Can your write soon our friend old ladys Peggy T. was here at day hab. Love, sister Peggy T. Write soon.*

And:

> *To Mrs. Dorothy K,*
> *Thank you for the holiday drink you gaveing me this holiday. I am very so-sorry that's I AT up this year in the dining room! I apologize for me! But I was happy your talked to me for your are so special today from me Miss Peggy T. I Love You so-so. Always you friend pen-pal.*

Peggy adores me and sometimes calls me "Sweets." One time she exclaimed, "Oh, I *love* this class, it's so worth the money!" (Obviously, she does not know that insurance pays the claims.) She uses her walker, as she is, according to herself, somewhat "wobbly." She complains frequently of "having a cold" and always asks me if she can remove her glasses when we work.

Peggy shoves all her possessions (art supplies, stationary, address books, old letters, newspapers, coupons, and money) into a *very* heavy purse (it might as well be a suitcase). She is a very generous person and constantly tries to give me some of these things as gifts. This includes leftover food from her lunch box, or things she has bought from vending. To say, "Peggy, you know I can't accept money or gifts or food" is to no avail. She is insistent to the point of driving me nuts. On top of that, she begs me for things, including things like greeting cards with pictures of cats, animal stickers, bookmarks, and magazines.

Peggy has a "boyfriend" named Henry. An older man, Henry is probably close to eighty years. According to Peggy, she and Henry met in a high-functioning group home years ago. Though she mentions him often, when they do see one another, it's as if she doesn't know him. Nick and I took them out to breakfast one time within the last year (Henry also uses a walker). Peggy complained most of the time about the conditions in the restaurant as well as about all the inside noise. Despite Henry bringing her a gift of fresh flowers, she basically ignored him during the entire meal. And despite Henry's history of residing in a high-functioning home, he appeared much more cognitively deficient than does she. I had to act shocked one time when she huffed into my room exclaiming, "Henry's messin' around!" (yeah, right). I later told Nick what she had said, and he came back with, "The only thing Henry's messin' around with is the remote."

Another hysterical scene with Peggy occurred at the day hab during a routinely scheduled fire drill. Unfortunately, the drill occurred when I was alone with her in the room. Peggy freaked out and panicked to no end. I tried and tried to get her to simply leave the building using her walker as she normally does. She continued to shriek, "I can't do it, I can't do it!" Once we exited the building, she dropped and walked on her knees, still upright, all the way to the safety zone. You can imagine how she looked.

Peggy can make such preposterous statements at times. I remember one time when I asked her what her middle name was; she immediately started speaking of the police and "having the death penalty given to me." I had no idea where that came from or how I had triggered it. From my understanding, she has had delusional ideas about herself being with the singer Glen Campbell (specifically, being married to and pregnant with his child). A couple of years ago, she was in a minor bus accident which had broken her nose. Later asking her about it, she said that she'd been taken to the hospital where they told her, "There is no chance for you to be saved."

Recently Peggy came into the room complaining, "This damned arthritis—I thought I was paralyzed this morning!" Lately she has experienced a great deal of anxiety about her pending colonoscopy. When I asked her when it was going to be, she retorted with, "I wish they'd make up their damned minds—I almost died going under last time!" When I asked her recently about the new stationary she had purchased, she exclaimed, "It just up and frickin' disappeared!" Once in class she commented about how uncomfortable her new ladies' undergarments were and that maybe she "shouldn't be talkin' about that stuff in class—you know what I mean?"

One of Peggy's most humorous but profound comments was the day after the 2016 presidential election. She walked down the hall of the day hab, boldly stating, "It's too bad that Clinton lady lost. That man is going to hang us all!" When a couple of us laughed, she retorted back with, "I'm serious!" I tell you, she has true insight.

Perhaps the funniest thing I've ever heard *anyone* say occurred when she was telling me about a man she'd met in Amish country. She said the man supposedly knew me. When I tried to clarify with, "Are you sure he knows me?" she replied matter-of-factly, "Yes, he does. He's human, but he's got Amish in him." How could anyone even *make up* anything that funny?

Peggy reaches deep into my soul. One day she came in and passionately said, "Jessica, I really care about you." I knew she was speaking from her heart. Another time she told me, "If it wasn't for you, I'd be dumb." It meant more than I can tell you. It wasn't long after that when she said, "You're the only teacher that's kept me on this long," causing both of us to laugh.

Chapter 13

No Ray of Hope

Recently discharged from my speech therapy services is a young man named Ray. He came to us from another agency several years ago, having reached the age of twenty-one. Ray was a sad case from the start. His mother had abused alcohol during her pregnancy with him, and as a result he had fetal alcohol syndrome disorder. He was also diagnosed with: sensorimotor neuropathy (a progressive disorder of the peripheral nerves causing overall weakness), moderate ID, intermittent explosive disorder, impulse control disorder, psychotic disorder, seizure disorder, anxiety disorder, osteoporosis, and mitral valve insufficiency (blood flowing backward in the heart).

A good-looking man, Ray depends on a wheelchair to ambulate. He is slouched over in the chair most of the time. Ray is by nature friendly, and keenly aware of what happens in his surroundings. He is verbal, though his speech is slurred and difficult to understand. With his progressive disorder, this is only getting worse. I have had to continually remind him, "Use your words," when he merely nods his head or shrugs. He can carry on a simple discussion, asks a fair number of questions, but almost never initiates a topic himself.

Ray's ID is glaring. He can recognize most letters of the alphabet, but he cannot read even the simplest of words. I have worked with him for a long time on writing his first name. He can almost get it, but it never truly comes to pass. When writing anything, his letters are indecipherable, completely unable to be read.

Ray cannot state his correct age or date of birth. He can identify most colors and numbers one through nine. He can also identify several animals and appears to really *like* animals. He has enjoyed viewing some of my *Ranger Rick* magazines. He told me his favorite pastime was fishing and can name some specific types of fish, such as bass.

I also know that Ray really enjoys listening to country music, and that he's seen Garth Brooks onstage. And just for the record—Ray was in my room one day and, as he rarely does, initiated a conversation with, "I like that song." The song was "Hotel California" by the Eagles. Being a great fan of classic rock, I was impressed. That song had topped the charts years and years before he was even born.

Eating is a complete ordeal for Ray. He transfers from the wheelchair to an adaptive chair for meals, but he needs a chest support to stay upright. As his neuropathy intensifies, his overall posture continues to fail, and his head remains down most of the time. As part of having speech impairment, he drools. Ray is incontinent at times and certainly must be in a great deal of pain, though he doesn't complain.

Ray's weakness and lethargy deter his ability to eat. He was just recently downgraded from an all one-inch-pieces cut-to-size diet to an all one-half-inch-pieces and all-meats-ground-up diet. When he tires out at meals, or when it's difficult for him to use utensils, he must be fed by staff. It's nothing but a bad deal all around. His disorder affects both the nerves that supply feeling (sensory) and those that cause movement (motor). Subsequent results are not only difficulty with talking and swallowing, but also painful sensations in the arms and legs, overall weakness, cramps, spasms, and aches.

I saw Ray for speech therapy for several years. Even though his speech is deteriorating markedly, he was actually doing *well* in therapy class. We worked on the /l/ sound, and with models and prompts, he was much more apt to make the sound correctly. He would only tolerate very short sessions (ten minutes), however, and usually some sort of bribe was in order to get him to work even then. One of the bribes involved taking him to visit a staff of his choice for an additional ten minutes of talk. He seemed to really enjoy these conversations, but in the end, even that wasn't enough to keep him willing to continue to take part.

Let's face it, speech therapy is work—hard work. There is no way around that. Ray simply did not want to work for it. Whether or not the connotation of "speech therapy" embarrassed him, I am still not sure. He would never give me his reasoning. He continues to go to OT and PT, but I believe as these therapies involve using more exciting motor skills (such as by making cookies and being assisted to walk), he doesn't perceive them the same. I can make a man talk, but I can't made him walk.

I have conflicting feelings today about my experience with Ray. In one sense, I know he needs the help with his speech and can only benefit from such. On the other hand, why the farce? "Okay, Ray, we will send you to speech therapy for twenty minutes and patch you up, then send you down to OT to patch you up some more," and so on, and so on.

Ray will never be normal, and he knows it. I look into his eyes, and I know what he is thinking. I can see the anger, the anger that leads him to violent behaviors in the group home, in the day hab, and during visits to his foster home. One time he even ripped the shirt completely off a male staff member in the day hab (that staff immediately transferred to another site).

Ray just wants to jump out of that wheelchair and be a normal twenty-something-year-old guy. As long as he is on this earth, that will never happen. He will never go out on a date, get married, have sex, live independently, or hold a job. He will never even be able to use the *toilet* without assistance. None of this is okay, none of it is right, and most certainly, none of it is fair. He will never know any of the things we take for granted as the norm.

Instead of what I *have* done, what I *really* want to do is fall down on the floor and weep with him and *for him* because of his lot in this life. Then after weeping, maybe we could share a prayer or two. And while speaking of farce, why do we expect these people to do what we don't even do ourselves? Why can't we take them for who they are, instead of this incessant need to "program?" "Sit up straight, put your fork down between bites, chew thoroughly before you take another bite, don't talk while you're eating, blah, blah, blah, blah…" Why was I always *literally* in someone's face, trying to make him perform? I know, I know, attempting Utopia justifies our jobs, but sometimes it makes absolutely no sense.

Chapter 14

Let's Play Charades

One of my delights in active speech class is Dougie, a sweet man in his mid-fifties with anxiety disorder and severe ID. He has poor coping skills and difficulty regulating his feelings. Dougie has an acute phobia about sickness and medical care in general. This phobia is triggered if he feels ill or merely hears the mention of someone being sick.

Generally, Dougie has typical looks, though his tongue hangs out of his mouth most of the time. He is relatively slight in stature, with a short cropped "buzz cut." He fares well with individual staff, and he occasionally attempts to form bonds with his peers. I am unaware of any family members that he may have.

Dougie is essentially nonverbal, though he can say a few things perfectly, such as *Batman* and *Star Trek* (his main obsession and love). Dougie loves all action heroes and sci-fi, and he enjoys dancing and attending special events. He communicates largely through body language and facial expressions, and with gestures, he is really a champ.

I pick him up from his classroom once a week; we walk arm in arm down the hall, and he often kisses my hand. We usually work on sign language, and Dougie knows a fair amount of manual sign. He does, however, use many of his own substitute personal signs. While sometimes this is because he doesn't have the fine motor skills to make the signs correctly, often his are far better than the official signs. This is because of the special features he adds, and you will see this as I continue to describe.

The first time I showed Dougie a picture of a bird, I was left surprised. I was merely expecting him to flick his thumb and forefinger together, signifying a bird's beak. Instead, he mimed feeding a bird on his shoulder and he gave a bird whistle at the same time. Even better, when I presented him with a picture of a pigeon, he mimicked writing a little note, placed it in the talons of a bird, and then released the bird into the air. Finally, he lifted his hands and gave the carrier pigeon a wave goodbye.

All the more, I am fascinated by what Dougie pays attention to and what he can comprehend. If I show him a picture of a pasta dish or a pizza, he places his fingers to his lips, pulling them away, forming a loud kiss and vocalizing, "Mmm!!!" It's as if he is an Italian exclaiming, "Bene, molto bene!" He understands far more than is probably known.

If I show Dougie a picture of a mouse or a snake, he mimics placing the critter up my sleeve. One of the few things he can verbalize is, "Good girl," and he does so while pretending to pet a cat or a dog. Most recently, when I present him with a picture of a small dog, he starts to wring his hands as if he is the witch from *The Wizard of Oz* cackling, "I'll get you, my pretty, and your little dog too!" He howls for a wolf and snorts for a pig. For a sheep, he pretends to sew on his sleeve. Actually, this is very close to the true sign for "sheep," in which the fingers mimic the shearing of the animal's wool. For a deer, Dougie shouts, "Ho, ho, ho!" and puts his hands to his belly as if he is Santa Claus. When shown a picture of a shark, he points to his mouth. (I find this interesting, as he is intending to point to teeth, but he actually has no teeth.)

When Dougie sees a picture of a church, he makes a long, drawn-out "Oooooh" sound (which I take to represent the perception of a ghost). If he sees a mirror, he again wrings his hands (I take this to mean he is pretending to be the evil queen beseeching, "Mirror, mirror on the wall…"). When shown a picture of a motorcycle, he pretends to be "The Fonz," with thumbs-up and a long, drawn-out "Aayyyy!!"

Recently, our day hab held a contest to determine by votes which band or musical act was the all-time best. When over the loudspeaker it was announced that Michael Jackson had won, Dougie let out a no-uncertain "scoff" of a laugh, showing that he didn't agree with the results of that poll at all! Again, his comprehensive skills are keen, keener than one might assume.

Dougie does have a dark side, which I had been warned about from the start. I saw him become assaultive once, after his classroom aide told him six or seven times to cover his mouth when he coughed. Dougie went ballistic, kicking, hitting, and attempting to bite. The perpetual mention of something having to do with illness had set him off. It was awhile before I took him alone in the therapy room again. It all worked out for good though, as by working on sign language within his class, other staff, along with his peers, got to learn a bit of ASL.

Dougie is one whom I believe has "maxed out" as far as performance in therapy goes; I believe he has gone as far as he possibly can with me. He cannot sequence three-step pictures, identify colors, letters, or numbers, or count beyond ten. At one point I felt pressured by the treatment team to obtain a Dynavox for him. The team wanted to give him "speaking" skills, and so as far procuring the item went, I did. That had been a mistake. Dougie could not functionally use the device, nor was there any hope that he would be able to do so over time.

Dougie is who he is, and sometimes it gets repetitious and stale. It's the positive vibes and the smiles I get from him which end up making our sessions better than those just to grin and bear.

Nick and I had the privilege of attending Dougie's birthday party last year at his group home. Much to his delight, he received a real bingo game, where the little balls could be mixed and drawn from a jar. As the "caller," each time Dougie drew a ball, he would belt out "B-13!" that being the only letter-number combination he could speak. Despite his limitations, I truly believe that Dougie is one of our few individuals who has enjoyed life to its very max.

Chapter 15

That's Hard to Swallow

Eddie reappeared in my life a few years after I had known him in special group. To make a longer story short, he had been hospitalized one winter with pneumonia. Due to severe difficulties with swallowing, he had been downgraded from eating regular whole foods and drinking normal thin liquids by mouth. Instead, he had to be fed with a feeding tube three times a day. Upon discharge, he was transferred to a medical home (where an LPN is always present), and he had to leave his current house. I felt so badly for him. I mean, he was only thirty-six years old. Nonetheless, this was very real. After some time, I was called upon to implement a "Return to Oral Feed." That was a plan to administer swallow therapy and then to *slowly* begin a reintroduction to eating and drinking by mouth.

Eddie continued to be a wise guy, and he often made me laugh. Upon his relocation, we held a big meeting for him with all his treatment team at hand. Eddie had prepared a four-page list of new personal requests. Some of what he asked for was normal, such as a CD player and an iPad. Other requests were either outrageous, hilarious, or both. First, he listed an entire page of desired foods (what could we do with that?). It got even better when he asked us for a pet snake. He not only wanted a snake; he wanted both a male and a female snake so he could breed little snakes in his new home. Members of the team rolled their eyes and tried to stifle their laughs.

As far as treatment went, my job was to see Eddie twice weekly for swallow therapy "class." Meanwhile home staff were supposed to lead him in extra oral-motor drills three times a day. Though he was willing to work with me, Eddie gave the house staff a difficult time. He would yell and scream and deliver a deluge of swear words, almost without fail. Staff reported to me that Eddie would not do his oral exercises apart from sticking out his tongue and asking "How's that?"

Eddie and I worked at the dining room table in the home. He often interjected his quick wit. On one occasion we were doing the "Push-Pull Phonation." We completed this by placing our hands underneath our chairs, pulling up hard, and then producing and prolonging vowel sounds while we exhaled. The theories behind this conclude that the exercise strengthens muscles in the larynx (which houses the vocal cords), and that airway closure then increases during a swallow. The first time we did this, we prolonged "aaaaaaaa," "eeeeeee," "iiiiiiiiii," "oooooo," and "uuuuuu." Eddie then blurted out, "And sometimes 'y'!!!" You see what I mean.

At our first session after the team had met, Eddie carried on about the acquisition of the snakes. He went into greater detail this time: He wanted to crossbreed a boa constrictor and a python. I told him I didn't think that was possible; he continued to insist that his staff had told him that it was. The nuts and bolts of all this, however, was that Eddie couldn't eat, and he was suffering psychologically. On one of our therapy days, staff thoughtlessly tossed a hot takeout pizza right onto the table in our midst. Eddie had to get up and leave the room, muttering, "That's one of my favorite foods."

After several weeks of therapy, my new mission at that point was to return Eddie back to normal eating by mouth. It was one of the most tedious and undesirable tasks that I'd faced while at my job. Eddie and I endured one long, hot summer together. Food and drink had to be reintroduced in a painstakingly conservative fashion. To start, the foods had to be pureed and the liquids had to be pudding thickened. I started out by giving him only two ounces of each. I had to watch for signs of aspiration, such as coughing, nose running, watery eyes, and/or a wet, gurgly quality of voice. His temperature also had to be recorded directly before eating and then one hour later (a temperature spike can be indicative of food or drink in the lungs).

By the summer's end, Eddie was consuming more liberal quantities of both food and drink. Slowly over time, the consistencies had changed: foods went from pureed to ground to one-half-inch pieces to one-inch pieces, while liquids went from pudding thick to honey thick to nectar thick. It was time for Eddie to have a Modified Barium Swallow (MBS). This is a radiographic test designed to determine the causes of an impaired swallow. He underwent the test and his swallow had greatly improved; he was upgraded back to regular foods. Due to some remaining aspiration with thin liquids, however, he was upgraded only to nectar-thick drinks. Eddie's feeding tube was removed, and he moved back to his original home. Victory had been nearly complete.

To make another very long story shorter, Eddie gave staff a difficult time about the liquids, refusing often to drink them nectar thick. This became the battle of the wills. Some months later, and upon his demand, Eddie went back for a subsequent MBS. That time the verdict was such: Eddie could either drink the nectar-thick liquids or he could drink normal thin liquids while performing a technique called the *chin tuck*. The theories behind the chin tuck are: (1) the chin tuck position moves the back of the tongue closer to the back of the throat, helping to push both food and drink down, and (2) the chin tuck position narrows the entrance to the airway, reducing the risk of food and drink going into the lungs. Eddie continued to be obstinate and refused to do the chin tuck, but also refused to consume the thicker drinks. For reasons other than eating and swallowing, Eddie relocated to a different home in a different region, to a house not assigned to me. The last that I heard was that he was still giving the staff difficulty about the drinks. Some things just don't change.

Just as Eddie and I had reconnected due to a swallowing impairment, when I least expected it, Kurt also reentered my life for the very same cause. The IFEAST team had been called on to observe Kurt eat, because according to his staff, he showed the signs of aspiration. After observing him coughing at meals and learning that he'd had three or four recent bouts with pneumonia, we recommended an MBS. We as the team members thought that perhaps nectar-thick liquids might be recommended as a solution. It turns out that had been an overly optimistic thought. Just as with Eddie, Kurt's diet was downgraded from a regular one to a feeding tube. He had demonstrated gross aspiration with both liquids and solids, without a protective cough response. The SLP at the hospital made it clear that she believed the prognosis, even with swallowing therapy, was grim. (At first, Kurt's family had refused the nothing-by-mouth recommendation, but after his subsequent bouts with pneumonia, they succumbed to the idea of the tube.)

Meanwhile, Kurt's physical state had deteriorated quickly. He was very weak and uncoordinated and had to rely on a wheelchair in lieu of his legs. He drooled often, was sluggish, unresponsive, and generally just plain "spaced out." I wondered if the eight psychotropic drugs he was on had brought all of this, including the dysphagia, to pass. (The term *dysphagia* is defined as an impairment of the swallow.)

Nonetheless, I provided Kurt with the swallow therapy twice a week, just as I had done with Eddie. Surprisingly, he handled the entire ordeal quite well, and readily participated in the sessions. He, just as Eddie had been, was required to relocate to a medical home. Meanwhile, new adjustments to his medications had been made; he could somewhat walk again and could function better overall. Also, his drooling had completely disappeared.

Kurt had his therapy sessions at the day hab. I was always unclear as to whether or not he was doing his exercises at home. Anyway, he could be heard regularly from inside the building, swearing and screaming as his staff lead him from the outside onto the site. He was unsteady, and when staff held his gait belt, just as with Patrick, it was as if Kurt was on a leash.

Kurt repeated the MBS after the months of the swallow therapy, and the second results were just as poor as the first. He showed severe aspiration on all food and drink consistencies that were tried. He was only thirty-seven years old and told that he would probably need a feeding tube for the rest of his life. The therapy I had provided could not touch the underlying neurological impairments that stemmed from his childhood TBI. Our sessions were done. I was fit to be tied and can only imagine how he must be dealing with this over time. I was told that he often tries to sneak drinks and snatch coffee and water at day program as well as at home. I'm afraid not every tale ends as a fairy tale.

Chapter 16

It's Just a Game

It's interesting how some of the things that I have seen over the years have stayed inside my mind. Once when I was on the campus, I walked into one of the classrooms, and saw everyone engrossed in a giant jigsaw puzzle. This wasn't your typical eye-pleasing puzzle, however. The resulting picture was simply that of watermelons, sliced with pink pieces and seeds all around. Not being much of a fan of puzzles anyway, every piece looked like every other piece, and it drove me crazy to look at all those seeds. All I could think was, *Die, die, that wretched puzzle just makes me want to die*—and I was serious. And at some point, later on, just when I felt it was safe to go back into that room, I walked in, and they were doing that miserable puzzle *again*. God help me.

An intriguing person I met (while evaluating him for an IFEAST) was a math savant named George. Autistic with moderate ID following hypoxic brain injury at birth, George was also diagnosed with impulse control disorder, attention deficit, and Raynaud's syndrome (a rare disorder of vessels of the blood).

The mundane part of the story is that the team recommended George remain on a one-half-inch-pieces cut-to-size diet. The intriguing part of the story involved George's numerical skills. I presented him with a multiplication problem on paper: 2,156 × 13 to be precise. He took his time and solved the problem just as would you or I, with all the numbers written out. He came up with the correct value of 28,028. His accompanying staff also told me that George had a knack for determining the root of a square. The next problem that I presented him with asked that he derive the square root of 13. I will admit that even though he was not entirely correct, he still impressed me to a large degree. He wrote down "3.0055512"; the right answer is "3.6055512." I decided to give him a second chance and asked that he determine the square root of 3. He immediately wrote "1.7320508," which was entirely correct! How did he do that? How could he determine that in his head to the correct seventh decimal place? How did his brain truly work?

*****

Steven, who was a regular member of special group (and also the one who had voted for McCain), is a student whom I currently see. He is diagnosed with intermittent explosive disorder and moderate ID; he is also quite gregarious and verbose. Unfortunately, he loves to mutter his verbiage a great deal under his breath. As far as that goes, I've been unable to influence any change. Steven wears glasses, is quite tall, and very thin. His posture is abysmal; he walks stooped over all the time and when I work with him, he sits with his head nearly all the way down on the desk. As with the muttering, no amount of prompting brings any alteration to that.

As far as I know, Steven has no family that is actively involved. There is a woman he refers to as "my mother" whom on holidays he occasionally sees. I am not sure of their actual connection. As is typical, Steven is a loner, having little to do with peers but relishing interaction with staff. Once after giving him a special compliment, he made direct eye contact with me for the first and only time. He had turned and grinned from ear to ear, looking me squarely in the face; that was a onetime image forever imprinted on my brain.

Steven has always seemed to like me, and has really enjoyed our class. I believe that he delights in learning, though he cannot always retain information for long. We have completed lessons about animals, sports, and geography, and he responds well to exercises using maps. Steven will read a passage aloud (ranging from a grade-two to a grade-four level), and then try to answer questions on a quiz (fill-in-the-blank, true/false, and multiple-choice). At times he aces the answers, and at times I realize that nothing has truly sunk in. We will go back to the passage again and again, but often that is to no avail. I came to realize that Steven's medications greatly affect his skills; he performed miserably when lithium had been prescribed.

At one time, I was seeing Steven in his home, and it was always at the table right after he'd had a meal. One of our favorite activities was playing the "capitals game." I would name a capital city, and Steven would try to recall the corresponding state. It's funny; he always got nineteen out of fifty correct, and it was always the same nineteen. What was odd was that he could never get the two most obvious states—both Indianapolis and Oklahoma City contain the name of their respective states. No matter how many times I tried to stress that, each time one of those cities came up, he continued to draw a blank.

Steven is amusing and often exaggerates or overreacts. Once, when we were at the breakfast table, one of his housemates (a very large and strong woman) came up and hit him forcefully in the face. He darted from the table, shouting, "She broke my jaw!" He was uninjured but distraught, and unfortunately, our session was done. (I, however, had to formally attest to the incident that I'd personally witnessed.)

Most recently, we've been working on short stories from the Bible. *Bible Adventures* has lessons that seem to match his reading level exactly (whether or not they are cognitive matches remains a debate). Each story is presented on seven different cards; Steven reads these aloud. I then select target vocabulary words that have appeared in the text while asking him to summarize the basic plots. I've had to bite my tongue on several occasions at question time. When I asked him the fate of Daniel in the lion's den, he replied, "The lion ate him." Also, according to Steven, Jonah was killed by the whale. Well, I've tried. I've also developed the patience of Job (not coincidentally, another Bible man).

One session with Steven within the last year moved me deeply. He read his seven-page Bible story perfectly and answered every question just the same. I had tears rolling down my face when I told him, "That's the best job you have ever done." I was so proud of him.

Another one of my current students is a higher-functioning, very verbal woman named Rose. She is of small stature, with short black hair and olive-colored skin. Rose has Down syndrome, bipolar depression disorder, OCD, chronic kidney disease, anxiety, and moderate ID.

Rose first came to our agency at the age of forty, living at home with her elderly parents up to then. She is the youngest of several children; her parents are immigrants from Southeast Asia. It was remarkable discovering that a moderately intellectually disabled person such as Rose could actually converse in two tongues. Rose can speak the language of the "old country" as well as she can talk in English. To me, that is a unique and special thing.

JESSICA WISLEY

Rose had been a codependent while still living at home, looking to her mother to even be fed by a spoon. She'd had a job at a vocational workshop but basically refused to go because her mother could not attend. Rose refused to leave her bed, dress herself, or bathe.

Some of Rose's compulsions are: the continual making and remaking of her bed, untying and retying her shoes, licking her empty plate repeatedly, and arranging and rearranging her coloring books until they're completely straight on the shelf. I first worked with Rose within her group home; there I witnessed her refuse to take off her hat and coat when she arrived home. She often refused for hours to relinquish her lunch box, talk, or move. I know at other times she refuses to eat unless certain favorite staff are there. At other times she refuses to go to bed, falling down on the living room floor instead.

Most recently, staff have had to deal with Rose's obsessions with the coloring books, as she steals them from her day hab and housemates' rooms. Consequently, staff have had to implement a restriction of only three pages to color per day. Rose has asked me multiple times for such books; once long ago I had given her some, but then learned that it would ultimately lead to nothing good.

More recently, I have worked with Rose in our agency's day hab after hours; she is dropped off there every Monday afternoon. She is always happy to see me, and usually we hug. We work on very simple reading, writing, and spelling. Despite her limitations, Rose can read a few basic words, and we rely on *Ranger Rick* for our lessons. Though she retains nothing from the information about the animals, I honestly believe she enjoys the sessions as a whole. She is fairly adept at recognizing target words by lessons' ends and can actually define a few of the words. She has recently grasped the concept of ending words with the letters "ing." Rose is sweet and loves to learn, and therein lies the reward. She is a personal delight.

Every week without fail Rose tells me the same thing: "I talked to my sister last night, and I told her you were really beautiful." I then ask, "And what did she say?" Rose invariably replies with a smile, "Oh, she just laughed." Then she repeats the story, this time with her brother described as being on the other end of the phone. As I stated previously, I will take my compliments when, where, and from whom I can. I couldn't adore her to any greater degree.

After our lesson, it is usually thirty minutes or so until Rose's staff can arrive and take her home. Rose and I decided we would play checkers during the wait. Quite honestly, it is something I anticipate. Despite her limitations, Rose is a competitive and determined lady, and she continues to build her game-playing skills. Fairly often I feel it is my duty to try to let her win. Have you ever attempted to rig checkers so that your opponent wins? Despite all my efforts ("Is that a good move?", "Which piece is in danger?", "Try to corner my piece," etc.), I almost always end up as the victor. It's not easy to *let* someone win! Try it sometime.

Chapter 17

All in Good Faith

One morning I went to work and Rachael asked me if I knew that Barry had died the night before. I was shocked. He had choked on a piece of roast beef. First responders had been summoned, and the Heimlich maneuver performed, but all to no avail. He was gone.

I was fortunate enough to attend the funeral, and I tried unsuccessfully to stifle back my tears. At the end, a group of us from work walked up to the coffin to render a final salute. I spoke to Barry's father and told him what a pleasure Barry had been to know. His dad's face was worn, but appreciative and kind. In a stark contrast, from one of Barry's cousins, I got the coldest and nastiest of glares. She did not know me from Eve. All I could think was that she had declared me guilty by my association through my job. For what had happened, I got the distinct impression that she blamed us all.

I look back at my journal; I had written that I felt it was sad that Barry would never live a normal life. Other than existing in the group home, he would aspire to little more. I suppose the question will always remain: Did Barry intentionally try to choke, overstuffing his mouth with grave intent? We will never know, but whatever is the case, I honestly believe that Barry is in a better place, basking in a world void of sorrow and pain.

*****

As much as I feel there was a reason to have served in the role I have for so long, I still admit I continue to have my share of despair. I will say that when I see Peggy's independent writing, it can be discouraging for sure. Nothing's coherent, and it's as if she's never had a day of instruction in her life. After five years, I wonder if I've even helped her at all. What had I gone back to school for? What was the point? Sometimes I feel like I'm just spinning my wheels, and sometimes I question the purpose of my position itself.

I am also thinking of one student named Matt, whom I have worked with for several years. I have been trying to teach him the category concept, and I obtained a box game for him that targets related skills. The main idea involves taking small magnetic pictures and placing each of them within the group in which things are somehow alike. With this particular activity, the categories are animals, household items, objects that provide transportation, clothing, and foods.

I learned very quickly that Matt cannot tackle four or five categories at once. So then, I simplify things, handing him either a piece depicting an animal or a piece displaying a food. You would think by the law of averages, he would score at fifty percent. You definitely thought wrong. He has consistently performed with only thirty percent success. Sometimes I think Matt is just simply trying to fail.

I look back at some of my writing:

> *My depression deepens. Just more snow and cold. What does all of this mean in the master scheme of things? We've gone over the same things over and over—this is who he's going to be. Matt plateaued long ago. His family expects services for life and I can't let them down. There is no graduation from speech therapy for either the individuals or for me. It doesn't end like a semester or a school year or a term; no one moves on to a new teacher, a new concept or a new grade. This is prevailing travail for us all. Today's session was exasperation and I don't feel like recording any "progress" notes. What good for Larry comes by his learning words like aviation, wealthy, or team? How does it help him that he knows who invented the phone? What difference will it have made for him in the end? How was a treatment plan going to change his life?*

I'm so tired of being in people's faces, and I truly question how long I can continue to work with this group. It is the ones in that grey area for whom I feel the most concern. I'm speaking of those who are truly impaired but have the cognition to know how different and helpless they are. I'm talking also about those without severe deficits but know that neither will they ever be the "norm." Again, not being able to read is a big part of the dilemma for many, and those who can't read do attempt to hide that fact. I mean, if I had to face what some of these people face daily, I might be hiding myself too.

*****

Today, as I look back, I tally the pros and cons. Fortunately, I can come up with more pros than cons. Or is that something to regret? If there were more cons, I could more easily justify leaving, but now I can't do that. I've considered a recount, but realize that would be pointless, as the results would be just the same.

I've even become acclimated to the IFEAST part of the job, and other than the dreaded feeding tubes, that part I can actually embrace. (In fact, there was a time when I felt my role on the dysphagia team was the *only* beneficial thing I had done.) Despite the feelings of uselessness with the cases in which I see no growth, there is so much that I truly *have* liked. So much has brought me great inspiration, such as listening to Peggy's funny anecdotes, the success with Jerry and Pete, and the weekly checkers game with Rose. Is it the right time to move on? In many ways, I really do want to press on. I want to devote the following chapters of my life (in both a figurative and a literal sense) to telling these particular tales.

As I'm about to retire, there is much that I now know. During the days (and even years) when I despised my job, it was because I looked down on the people I served. They weren't ever going to be "normal" or be tomorrow's leaders, and I resented that inside. It's when I finally realized that *they* are God's people *too*, the very same as I, that my entire psyche transformed overnight. I actually stopped despising my career field and actually ceased loathing my life.

Had I made a difference? There had been *some* growth with *some* of the individuals *some* of the time. No, it wasn't the treatment goals or any formal objective that changed the master plan. No, they would never be the leaders of future days. The point was that someone *cared* about them, that someone from the outside thought they were worth enough to pay attention to, that maybe he or she had a thought that was worth a dime. I hated my job during each of the days I went into it with the subconscious sentiment that we as "normal" are somehow the best. But there really is no difference between any of them and me. They are here for specific purposes, just as certainly am I. My entire perspective changed once I was willing to acknowledge that. I was no better—*no one* is better.

I found a new satisfaction in realizing that it was an honor to belong to their club. I can now embrace a social outcast with as much passion as if I'd met the Queen. No one should be "written off," as we *all* have redeeming sides. It works two ways; it was a blessing for *me* having people care about *me* during some of the very low and lonely points in my life. I feel this was one of the reasons I'd been in this place to start. I believe that some things in this world are simply designed to unfold.

It's not really about what's *out there*; it's about what's *in here* that truly takes the cake. *Here* is the center of the world; *here* is where things are happening, and surely *here* is our finest hour. I learned that we get so wrapped up in wanting to be *out there* in the world, doing things grandiose, that we forget what this moment is actually all about.

No, it isn't about a formal objective or any target goal. It's about things on a much deeper plane. It's about getting Ray a cup of water when he needed to quench his thirst. It's about sitting and listening to "Hotel California" together after buying him *The Eagles Greatest Hits* CD. It's about the "high five" shared with Pete when he'd exclaimed, "I did it, you see?!!" It's about a low-functioning man telling me, "I'm glad you're here," when the electricity went out in his home.

ALL THOSE PIECES

It's about Charles waiting for me in suit and tie, ready to go to church. It's about him *independently* writing me a card saying, *I bring you love and joy.* It's about the Good Samaritan lesson, with my students on the floor. It's about Wayne giving the thumbs-up sign, then waving from across the field. It's about all those pieces—those bits. It's about that look from across the room, that smile from Alice who's lived through hell. It's that smile that says, *Yes indeed, it's me, see?!!* It's about Jerry's earnest eyes, pleading forgiveness for yesterday's deeds. It's about something that transcends, that reaches beyond all of the thinking we've ever known. It's about meeting one another on the walkway at our common human core. That's what it's all about, and that is what I unknowingly fell back on during the days I despised my life. After all, wasn't it Jesus who said, "When you did it for the least of these my brothers, you did it for me?"

Epilogue

My thoughts entertain me during the final months of the job. I think back to all the good that has happened and that continues to come to pass. I saw Wayne recently at one of our individual's funerals; he was as proud as I was when I introduced him to Nick. I smiled when I found Alice's U.S. map in my files, with some of the states colored in. I think back to funny incidents, such as one of my unintelligible students who suddenly *could* be understood when he began talking about his brother's "no-good wife from Cleveland."

I think back to all the idiosyncrasies that consumed so many people on grounds. For example, I think about watching Edmund rearrange sticks on the campus in order to make them align. I think back to Charles demanding a thousand copies of his shopping list. I'm also pleased when I remember the many comments from staff telling me how much they'd gotten out of learning how to sign. I'm proud when I hear them tell me how well I work *with* people, rather than simply working around them. I think back with satisfaction when one of the retiring classroom aides said to me, "Jessica, you're a very good woman." I remember her squeezing my arm as she left the schoolhouse for the very last time.

Larry continues to surprise me often. Just recently, I gave him ample cues and prompts, and he actually had a normal conversation with me. For him, that's really a new and a profound thing. He told me with details what he had done at program that day and what he had done at the fair. I asked him as to his favorite band, and without hesitation he said, "KC and the Sunshine Band." I asked him to guess *my* favorite band, and he again with no reservation said, "Billy Joel" (*interesting*, I thought to myself). I said, "No, take another guess," to which he then replied, "The Average White Band." (Where on earth did he come up with *that* one?) When I told him to take a third guess, he could not be understood, so I just came right out and told him my favorite band was Jethro Tull. Based on his lack of response, I gathered that was a name with which he was not familiar. I said, "They sing 'Aqualung,' 'Bungle in the Jungle,' and 'Thick as a Brick.'" We will see what he retains of that. (I did have to make sure that he knew the proper name was "Jethro Tull" and not "Jefro Tull.")

Peggy continues to entertain me beyond belief. I joined her on a field trip to an Amish cheese factory on her birthday earlier this year. She talked *incessantly* in the van, one full hour there and one full hour back. She described how her father used to "breed cows" by sticking his hands inside of them. She also stated, "The Amish have nice complexions, are bashful, and they also wear shoes" followed by, "The Amish are fussy and they choose their wives at auctions." Right now, she is learning how the numbers correspond to the months; she has a big grin on her face as we begin every letter writing session with "January—one! February—two!" and so on and so on.

Recently she said to me, "I was going to get mad at you once, then I told myself 'She's not someone I want to lose.'" I said, "Right choice!" as I chuckled to myself. Peggy also knows that Nick and I are planning on getting married early next year. She asked me, "You aren't leaving here after that, are you?" (As of yet, she does not know about my plans to retire.) I said, "I'm not sure, we'll see. But they'll replace me if I leave." To that she replied, "The new person won't be as nice as you; you're the best friend that I have." She followed up with, "I don't think I'll go to speech class anymore if you leave. You definitely give me strength." I think that speaks for itself.

Just yesterday I drove past one of the group homes near the campus and saw Nate walking home. I rolled down my window to simply say hello. Nate came running to the car quickly, exclaiming, "I wanna come back! I wanna learn how to read! I won't skip no more!" That touched me more than I can say. Today I opened my mail to find speech referrals for both Ray and Tom. The latter reads, *Tom wants to know what he might work on, as he hasn't had speech therapy for some time.* Suddenly everyone who fired me wants me back again.

A few weeks ago, in one of our office buildings, I encountered Suzy, indirectly, again. This was the first time I'd seen her in about ten years. I overheard a conversation she was having with both her psychologist and a female staff. Suzy looked generally the same, although she was thinner and wore plastic glasses, which was something new.

The topic at hand was, of course, the incessant preoccupation with numbers. I heard Suzy say, "Sometimes talking about numbers makes me happy, and sometimes it makes me sad. I wanna stop talking about numbers altogether. I wanna do it on my own." Her psychologist replied, "You've shown that you can't do it on your own." Suzy continued to say, "I wanna stop talking about numbers altogether." As they adjourned and left the room, Suzy turned toward the elevator, looked back, and said, "I'm gonna show you I can do it," and I smiled to myself. It's all worth it in the end.

Every person with a disability is an individual.
—Itzhak Perlman

Afterword

About Developmental Disabilities

According to the May Institute, 15%—or one out of six children—ages three to seventeen will have one or more developmental disabilities in their lifetimes. Males are twice as likely to have a development disability than females. As the Centers for Disease Control reports, one child out of fifty-nine in the United States will now develop an autism spectrum disorder (boys are four times as likely to develop an ASD than are females). According to the National Institute of Health, autism in the United States increased 15% between the years of 2016–2018 (2.1% of children are affected). Children from families with income below the federal poverty level have an increased prevalence of developmental disabilities.

It is important to watch and determine whether or not your child is meeting the common developmental milestones. If your child is not meeting milestones for his or her age, then share your concerns with your physician or health-care professional. If treatment is needed, a better outcome is likely if you are early to intervene!

About Mental Illness

According to Mental Health America, 20% of adults (one out of five) in the United States will experience some sort of mental illness in their lifetimes. In the United States, the most common mental health disorder is anxiety, affecting over 42 million adults (21%). Depression affects 16 million adults, with about 7% of the population having at least one major depressive episode in the last year. Each year, almost 2% of the population is diagnosed with bipolar disorder, while there are over 4% diagnosed with post-traumatic stress disorder. Schizophrenia is present in 1% of the American population. Over 10 million of those afflicted with a mental illness also suffer from an addiction disorder. Additionally, more than one out of four homeless Americans suffer from some serious mental illness.

Unfortunately, only 15% of those afflicted will ever receive any kind of treatment for their mental illness. Stigma prevents open discussion of mental illnesses, and lack of understanding prevents the afflicted from seeking treatment. Often, the individual experiencing the mental illness becomes blamed for his or her problem. Clearly open discussion and eliminating the stigma and blame are needed for millions to seek the help and treatment they need.

ALL THOSE PIECES

About Illiteracy

The International Communication Project reports that 800 million adults worldwide (two-thirds being female) lack minimum literacy skills. According to Matthew Brennan ("The Link Between Illiteracy and Incarceration," 2018) every one out of four children in the United States grows up without learning how to read. Even more sobering is the fact that 66% of students who cannot read by the end of the fourth grade end up going to jail. The Literacy Project Foundation reports that 60% of prison inmates are functionally illiterate. Of those who are released from prison, 70% return without having obtained significant literacy help (Brennan). Clearly there is a direct correlation between illiteracy and incarceration.

The American Speech and Hearing Association (ASHA) lists several early warning signs of reading and writing problems in children: lack of interest in shared book reading, persistent baby talk, difficulty understanding simple directions, difficulty learning or remembering names of letters, and/or failure to recognize or identify letters in the child's own name. If you have concerns about your child's emergent literacy skills or speech and language development, please contact a certified speech-language pathologist or contact ASHA directly at asha.org or call 800-638-8255.

Acknowledgements

I would like to thank Nick, for without you, the technical elements of this endeavor would have been much more difficult. Even more, I thank you for all your continued love, inspiration, and support while I completed this book.

I thank all my family and all my friends who have helped me over the years to continue to seek my dreams.

Thank you to all my teachers who encouraged me to excel.

Kudos to all my fellow workers—I love you all.

Most of all, I thank every developmentally-disabled person I've had the privilege to serve. Without you, my life would have been incomplete.

APPENDICES

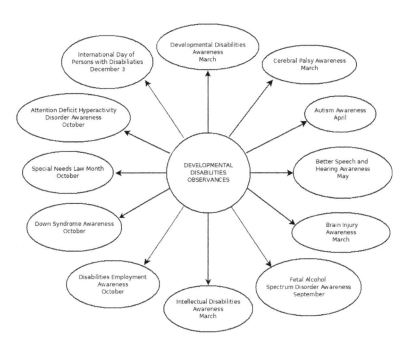

ALL THOSE PIECES

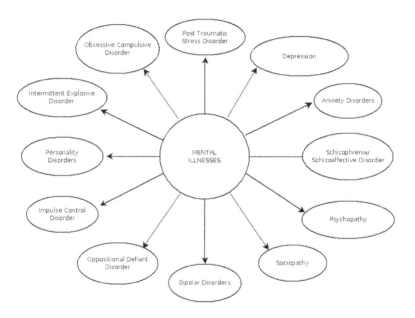

JESSICA WISLEY

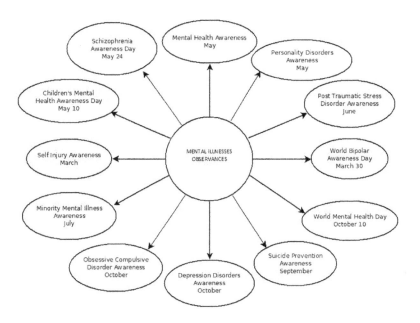

Glossary

advocacy. Public support for or recommendation of a particular policy or cause.

American Sign Language (ASL). The primary sign language used by deaf and hearing-impaired people in the United States and Canada.

anxiety disorder. Chronic, exaggerated worry about everyday routine life events and activities, lasting at least six months, almost always anticipating the worst. This disorder may be accompanied by fatigue, trembling, headache, and/or nausea.

articulation. The foundation of clear and distinct sounds in speech; the way in which words are pronounced.

Asperger's syndrome. The condition that doctors call a "high-functioning" type of autism spectrum disorder (ASD). Asperger's syndrome symptoms are less severe than in other kinds of ASDs.

aspiration. The accidental intake of food particles or liquids into the lungs, often leading to aspiration pneumonia.

asthma. A condition in which a person's airways become inflamed, narrow, and swell, making it difficult to breathe.

attention deficit hyperactivity disorder (ADHD). Any of a range of behavioral brain disorders occurring primarily in children, including such symptoms as hyperactivity, impulsivity and poor concentration.

autism. A complex, neurobehavioral condition that includes impairments in social interaction and developmental language/communication skills, combined with rigid, repetitive behaviors.

autism spectrum disorder (ASD). A large spectrum of disorders that include impairments in social interaction and developmental language and communication skills. ASD includes both autism and Asperger's syndrome.

bilateral. Having or relating to two sides; affecting both sides. For example, a bilateral hearing loss affects both ears.

bipolar. A brain disorder that causes unusual shifts in mood, energy, activity levels, and the ability to carry out day-to-day tasks. Bipolar is also known as manic-depressive illness.

borderline personality (BP). A serious, mental illness characterized by pervasive instability in moods, interpersonal relationships, self-image, and behavior.

central auditory processing disorder (CAPD). A disorder occurring when the brain's ability to filter and interpret sounds is impaired. People with CAPD are able to hear but have difficulty organizing and processing information. They may also have difficulty discriminating between different sounds

and difficulty comprehending speech when background noise is present.
cerebral palsy (CP). A neurological disorder caused by a nonprogressive brain injury or malformation that occurs while a child's brain is developing. CP affects body movement and muscle coordination.
chorea. A movement disorder marked by involuntary spasmodic movements, especially of the limbs and facial muscles. Chorea is typically symptomatic of neurological dysfunction.
cleft lip and cleft palate. Opens or slits in the upper lip, the roof of the mouth (palate), or both. Cleft lip and cleft palate result when facial structures that are developing in an unborn baby don't completely close.
clozapine. An antipsychotic drug used as a sedative and for treatment-resistant schizophrenia.
conduct disorder. A repetitive and persistent pattern of behavior in children and adolescents in which the rights of others or basic social rules are ignored.
congenital. Of a disease or physical abnormality present from birth; inborn, inherited, and/or hereditary.
constipation. A condition in which there is difficulty in emptying the bowels.
day habilitation. A community-based program designed to help people with developmental disabilities lead more independent and productive lives, through

building and maintaining socialization and self-help skills.

darifenacin. Medication used to treat urinary incontinence.

deaf. Lacking or deficient in the sense of hearing; unable to hear.

deep brain stimulation. A neurological procedure involving the implantation of a medical device called a neurostimulator which sends electrical impulses to specific targets in the brain for the treatment of movement disorders, including Parkinson's disease and dystonia.

delusions. False beliefs; mistaken beliefs held with strong conviction even in the presence of evidence to the contrary.

depression. A common and serious mood disorder that causes a persistent feeling of sadness and loss of interest.

diabetes. A chronic disease caused by inherited and/or acquired deficiency in production of insulin by the pancreas, or by the ineffectiveness of the insulin produced.

dialectical behavior therapy (DBT). A therapy providing individuals with new skills to manage painful emotions and decrease conflict in relationships.

Down syndrome. A congenital disorder arising from a chromosome defect, causing intellectual impairment and physical abnormalities including short stature and a broad facial profile.

Dynavox. A portable, electronic speech-generating device manufactured by *Tobii Dynavox* (formerly *Mayer-Johnson Dynavox*) used to assist individuals in overcoming speech, language, and learning challenges (Pittsburgh, PA).

dysfluency. The impairment of the ability to produce smooth, fluent speech, as by a pause or repetition of a word or syllable. Stuttering is one form of dysfluency.

dyslexia. A specific language disability that is neurobiological in origin. It is characterized by difficulties with accurate and/or fluent word recognition and by poor spelling and decoding skills.

dysphagia. Difficulty or discomfort in swallowing due to abnormal nerve or muscle control.

dystonia. A movement disorder characterized by sustained or intermittent muscle contractions causing abnormal, often repetitive movements or postures.

encephalitis. Inflammation of the brain tissue.

epilepsy. A disorder of the central nervous system, characterized by either mild, episodic loss of attention or sleepiness (petit mal seizures), or by severe convulsions with loss of consciousness (grand mal seizures).

esophageal. Having to do with the esophagus, which is the part of the alimentary canal that connects the throat to the stomach. In humans the esophagus is a muscular tube lined with mucous membrane.

fetal alcohol spectrum disorder (FASD). An "umbrella" term used to describe the range of effects that can occur in an individual with prenatal alcohol exposure. These effects can have lifelong implications, including physical, mental, behavioral, and other learning deficiencies.

frequency. The number of waves that pass a fixed place in a given amount of time. The Hertz (Hz) measurement is the number of waves that pass by per second. A person who has hearing in the normal range can hear sounds that have frequencies between 20 and 20,000 Hz.

gastro esophageal reflux disease (GERD). A long term condition where acid from the stomach rises up into the esophagus.

GED. General Educational Development or Graduate Equivalency Degree. A series of tests to determine if a person has a high school level of education. A certain score is needed to pass.

guardian. A person who looks after and is legally responsible for someone who is unable to manage his/her own affairs, especially for an incompetent or disabled person.

gynecomastia. The enlargement of a man's breasts, usually due to hormone imbalance or hormone therapy.

hallucinations. Perceptions in the absence of external stimuli that have qualities of real perceptions.

hard-of-hearing (HOH). Refers to an individual who has a mild to moderate hearing loss who may communicate through sign language, spoken language, or both.

Harrington rod. A stainless-steel surgical device, historically implanted along the spinal column to treat curvature of the spine (scoliosis).

hearing impairment. A deficit in hearing, classified in terms of the severity and type of impairment. Severity is categorized based on the minimum sound that can be heard with the better ear. The higher the decibel (dB), the louder the sound.

Heller's syndrome (also known as childhood disintegration disorder). A rare pervasive developmental disorder occurring in late or later childhood, which results in the regression of abilities with language, social function, and/or motor skills.

hiatal hernia. The protrusion of an organ, typically the stomach, through the esophageal opening in the diaphragm. Larger hiatal hernias may cause acid reflux, heartburn, or difficulty swallowing.

hypoxic brain injury. A brain injury that occurs when the brain is deprived of oxygen.

impulse control disorder (ICD). A class of disorders characterized by impulsivity, failure to resist a temptation or urge, or the inability to not speak on a thought.

individual education plan (IEP). A document that is developed for each public-school child who needs special education. An IEP is tailored to the individual student's needs and must help teachers and related service providers to understand the student's disability and how the disability affects learning.

insulin. A natural hormone made by the pancreas that controls the level of the sugar glucose in the blood.

intellectual disability (ID). A disability originating before the age of eighteen, characterized by significant limitations in both intellectual functioning and in adaptive behavior, which covers everyday social and practical skills.

intellectual quotient (IQ). A total score derived from several standardized tests designed to assess human intelligence.

intelligible. A measure of how comprehensible speech is, or the degree to which speech can be understood.

intermittent explosive disorder (IED). A behavioral disorder characterized by explosive outbursts of anger and violence, often to the point of rage, that is disproportionate to the situation at hand.

language disorder. A communications disorder in which a person has persistent difficulties in learning and using various forms of language, such as spoken, written, or sign language. An individual with language disorder has language abilities that are significantly below those expected for his or her age, which limits his or her ability to communicate or effectively participate in many social, academic, or professional environments.

learning disability. A condition giving rise to difficulties in acquiring knowledge and skills to the level expected of those of the same age, especially when not associated with a physical handicap.

lisp. A speech defect in which the /s/ and /z/ sounds are pronounced like the /th/ sound.

lithium. A naturally occurring metal that in purified form is used to treat certain psychiatric disorders, especially bipolar disorder.

lorazepam. A benzodiazepine medication used to treat anxiety.

metoclopramide. A drug used to treat stomach and esophageal problems.

metoprolol. A prescription drug used to treat high blood pressure, angina, abnormal rhythms of the heart, and some neurological conditions.

mitral valve insufficiency. A disorder of the heart in which the mitral valve does not close properly when the heart pumps out blood, allowing blood to flow backward into the heart.

modified barium swallow (MBS) (also known as video fluoroscopic examination). A radiographic procedure designed to define the anatomy and physiology of a patient's oropharyngeal swallow in order to identify the cause of difficult or impaired swallowing.

mood disorder. A psychological disorder characterized by the elevation or lowering of a person's mood, such as depression or bipolar disorder.

neuropathy. A disease of one or more peripheral nerves, typically causing numbness or weakness.

obsessive-compulsive disorder (OCD). Repeated, intrusive, and unwanted thoughts or rituals that seem impossible to control.

occupational therapist (OT). A health rehabilitation professional working with those who need specialized assistance to lead independent and productive lives.

occupational therapy. The use of assessments and intervention to develop, recover, or maintain the meaningful activities or occupations of individuals. Occupational therapy may focus on increasing a person's ability to perform activities of daily living (ADL), including self-help skills and work.

olanzapine. An antipsychotic medication used to treat resistant depression.

oppositional defiant disorder (ODD). A disorder characterized by chronic aggression, hostility, disobedience, and defiance.

oropharyngeal. Having to do with the part of the throat that is at the back of the mouth, in contrast to nasopharyngeal (having to do with the part of the throat that is behind the nose).

osteopenia. Reduced bone mass of lesser severity than osteoporosis.

osteoporosis. A medical condition in which the bones become brittle and fragile from loss of tissue.

paranoid schizophrenia. The most common subtype of schizophrenia; a mental disorder characterized by abnormal behavior, strange speech, and a decreased ability to understand reality. Other symptoms include false beliefs, confused thinking, and hearing voices that don't exist.

paraphilia. A condition characterized by abnormal sexual desires, typically involving extreme or dangerous activities.

parasuicidal gesture. Self-harming behavior identified by the individual as suicidal but unlikely to actually result in death. Previous parasuicide is a predictor of suicide.

Peabody Picture Vocabulary Test—Revised (PPVT-R). A test of receptive vocabulary of Standard American English, intended to provide a quick estimate of the examinee's understanding of various words. (Dunn and Dunn, 1981).

pedophilia. A psychiatric disorder in which an adult has sexual fantasies about or engages in sexual acts with a prepubescent child.

pentosan. A weak blood thinner that is also used to treat bladder pain.

person-centered planning (PCP). An ongoing problem-solving process used to help people with disabilities plan for their futures. In PCP, groups of people focus on an individual and that person's vision of what he/she would like to do in the future.

personality disorder (PD). A deeply ingrained pattern of behavior that deviates markedly from the norms of generally accepted behavior, causing long-term difficulties in personal relationships or in functioning as part of society.

petit mal seizure. A form of epilepsy with very brief, unannounced lapses in consciousness and awareness.

pharynx. The membrane-lined cavity behind the nose and mouth, connecting them to the esophagus.

phobia. An extreme, disabling, and irrational fear of something that really poses little or no actual danger. Phobias lead to avoidance of objects or situations and can cause limitations of life.

phonemic awareness. The ability to hear and manipulate individual sounds.

phonological. Relating to the sounds in a particular language.

psychopathy. A kind of antisocial personality disorder characterized by persistent impaired empathy and amoral behavior along with the lack of ability to love or to establish meaningful personal relationships. A person with psychopathy typically has no conscience.

physical therapy (PT). Therapy for the preservation, enhancement, or restoration of movement and physical function that has been impaired or threatened by disease, injury, or disability.

post-traumatic stress disorder (PTSD). Persistent symptoms that occur after experiencing a traumatic event such as war, rape, child abuse, natural disasters, etc. Nightmares, flashbacks, depression, and angry, irritable feelings are common.

prevocational. Given or required before admission to a vocational school.

psychiatrist. A medical practitioner specializing in the diagnosis and treatment of mental illness.

psychologist. A professional specializing in diagnosing and treating diseases of the brain, emotional disturbances, and behavior problems.

psychotic disorder. A severe mental disorder that causes abnormal thinking and perceptions and a loss in touch with reality. Delusions and hallucinations are two main symptoms of psychotic disorder.

Raynaud's syndrome. A rare disorder of the blood vessels, usually in the fingers and the toes.

registered dietitian (RD). A regulated health-care professional licensed to assess, diagnose, and treat nutritional problems.

rubella. A contagious, viral disease with symptoms like mild measles. Rubella can cause fetal malformation or deafness in an unborn child if contracted in early pregnancy.

savant. A person with a mental deficit who has one or more genius-level abilities.

schizoaffective disorder. A mental disorder in which a person experiences a combination of schizophrenia symptoms, such as hallucinations or delusions, and mood disorder symptoms, such as depression or mania.

schizophrenia. A long-term mental disorder of a type involving a breakdown in the relation between thought, emotion, and behavior, leading to faulty perception, inappropriate actions/feelings, withdrawal from reality and personal relationships. Symptoms may include fantasy/delusion and a sense of mental fragmentation.

seasonal affective disorder (SAD). A subtype of depression or bipolar disorder that occurs around the same time every year. SAD typically occurs due to the decrease in natural lighting in the fall and winter in the Northern Hemisphere, though it can occur at other times of the year.

seasonique. A medication used to change a woman's bleeding pattern to produce either no periods or just four periods a year.

seizure disorder. A medical condition characterized by episodes of uncontrolled electrical activity in the brain (seizures). Seizure disorder may be hereditary or caused by birth defects or environmental hazards.

self-advocacy. The action of representing oneself or one's views or interests.

self-injurious behavior (SIB). The deliberate, repetitive, nonlethal harming of oneself; also termed self-mutilation or self-abuse.

sensorimotor. Of, relating to, or functioning in both sensory and motor aspects of bodily activity sensorimotor skills. Such skills involve the process of receiving sensory messages (sensory input) and producing a response (motor input).

sensorineural. Caused by a lesion or disease of the inner ear or the auditory nerve, especially as affecting hearing.

sertraline. A drug used to treat depression, obsessive-compulsive disorder, and panic/anxiety disorders.

sex offender. A person who commits a crime involving a sexual act.

sialorrhea. The excess production of saliva; hypersalivation; drooling.

sociopathy. A kind of antisocial personality disorder characterized by manipulating and callous behavior with little regard for others. A sociopath may have a propensity for untruthfulness and behavior that benefits the sociopath at the expense of others.

soft palate. The fold at the back part of the roof of the mouth that partially separates the mouth from the pharynx.

Sorensen Video Relay Service (SVRS). A manner in which deaf persons use a videophone (through a high-speed internet) to play SVRS calls to hearing persons who receive the calls on a standard phone; a type of videophone that assists deaf and hard-of-hearing people to communicate with others using sign language or a sign language interpreter (*Sorensen Communications,* Beavercreek, Ohio).

speech-language pathologist (SLP). A professional who evaluates and treats people who have deficits in speech or language.

speech-language pathology (SLP). A field of expertise practiced by a clinician known as a speech language pathologist, sometimes referred to as a speech therapist; the treatment for the improvement or cure of communication disorders, including speech, language, and swallowing disorders.

stuttering. Talking with continued involuntary repetition of sounds, especially initial consonants.

Stuttering Foundation of America (SFA). A nonprofit charitable organization working toward the prevention and improved treatment of stuttering (Memphis, Tennessee).

substance abuse. A harmful or hazardous use of psychoactive substances, including alcohol and drugs.

traumatic brain injury (TBI). A form of acquired brain injury, occurring when a sudden trauma causes damage to the brain.

thioridazine. An anti-psychotic medication used to treat psychotic disorders such as schizophrenia.

unintelligible. Not clear enough to be understood.

velar. Pronounced with the back of the tongue near the soft palate, as in /k/ and /g/ sounds in English.

visual impairment. A decreased ability to see to a degree that causes problems not corrected by usual means such as with eyeglasses or contact lenses. Visual impairments include blindness, night blindness, loss of central or peripheral vision, blurred vision, etc.

vocational. Related to or undergoing training in a skill or trade to be pursued as a career.

ziprasidone. An atypical antipsychotic drug used for the treatment of schizophrenia, acute mania, and bipolar disorder.

zonisamide. A drug used to control partial and other types of seizures.

Sources

American Speech-Language and Hearing Association, Rockville, MD.

Bible Trivia Game by Cadaco, 1999.

Brennan, Matthew. 2018, 3/25. *The Link Between Illiteracy and Incarceration.* Retrieved from https://matthewbrennancopywriter.com/illiteracy-and-incarceration/.

Centers for Disease Control and Prevention, Atlanta, GA.

Charlie and the Chocolate Factory. Directed by Tim Burton, 2005. Burbank, CA: Warner Bros. Pictures.

Child's Play. Directed by Tom Holland, 1988. Beverly Hills, CA: United Artists.

Dora the Explorer. Directed by George S. Chialtas, Gary Conrad, Henry Lenardin-Madden, Sherie Pollack, Arnie Wong. New York, NY: Nickelodeon.

Editors at Tangerine Press, The. 2005. *Funny Farm Joke Book.* First Edition. New York: Scholastic, Inc.

Editors at Tangerine Press, The. 2004. *Li'l Book O' Big Laughs.* First Edition. New York: Scholastic, Inc.

Great Bible Adventures. International Masters, 2002.

GQ. Conde Nast, New York, NY.

Hitch. Directed by Andy Tennant, 2005. Culver City, CA: Overbrook Entertainment.

https://internationalcommunicationproject.com/
https://onelinefun.com
Liar, Liar. Directed by Tom Shadyac, 1997. Hollywood, CA: Imagine Entertainment.
Lion King, The. Directed by Rob Minkoff and Roger Allers, 1994. Burbank, CA: Walt Disney's Pictures.
Literacy Project, The, Newport Beach, CA.
Lord of the Rings, The. Directed by Peter Jackson, 2001, 2002, 2003. Los Angeles, CA: New Line Cinema. Films.
May Institute, Randolph, MA.
Mental Health America, Alexandria, VA.
Meyer, Stephanie, 2005. *Twilight.* New York, NY: Little, Brown and Company.
Peabody Picture Vocabulary Test—Revised. Dunn and Dunn, 1981.
Ranger Rick. National Wildlife Federation, Reston, VA.
Sorensen Communications, Sorensen Video Relay Service. Beavercreek, OH.
Stuttering Foundation of America, The, Memphis, TN.
Tobii Dynavox (formerly Dynavox Mayer-Johnson). Pittsburgh, PA.
Wizard of Oz, The. Directed by Victor Fleming, 1939. Beverly Hills, CA: Metro-Goldwyn-Mayer.
Zondervan Corporation, The. 1999. *The New Testament with Psalms and Proverbs.* New International Version.

About the Author

Jessica Wisley is a speech-language pathologist residing in upstate New York. She received her master's degree at Buffalo State College and also holds college degrees from the Pennsylvania State University and Troy State University. Jessica spent fifteen of her twenty-year speech-pathologist career working with developmentally-disabled adults. She is also retired from the United States Air Force. Jessica has enjoyed creating stories since childhood. In addition to writing, she enjoys traveling and playing the piano. *All Those Pieces* is her first book. Jessica lives with her husband Nick and their cats.

CPSIA information can be obtained
at www.ICGtesting.com
Printed in the USA
LVHW111012111120
671389LV00007B/63